365 People Who Changed the World

Om KIDZ | Om Books International

Reprinted in 2022

Corporate & Editorial Office
A-12, Sector 64, Noida 201 301
Uttar Pradesh, India
Phone: +91 120 477 4100
Email: editorial@ombooks.com
Website: www.ombooksinternational.com

© Om Books International 2015

ISBN: 978-93-84225-34-6

Printed in China

10 9 8 7 6 5 4

Sales Office
107, Ansari Road, Darya Ganj
New Delhi 110 002, India
Phone: +91 11 4000 9000
Email: sales@ombooks.com

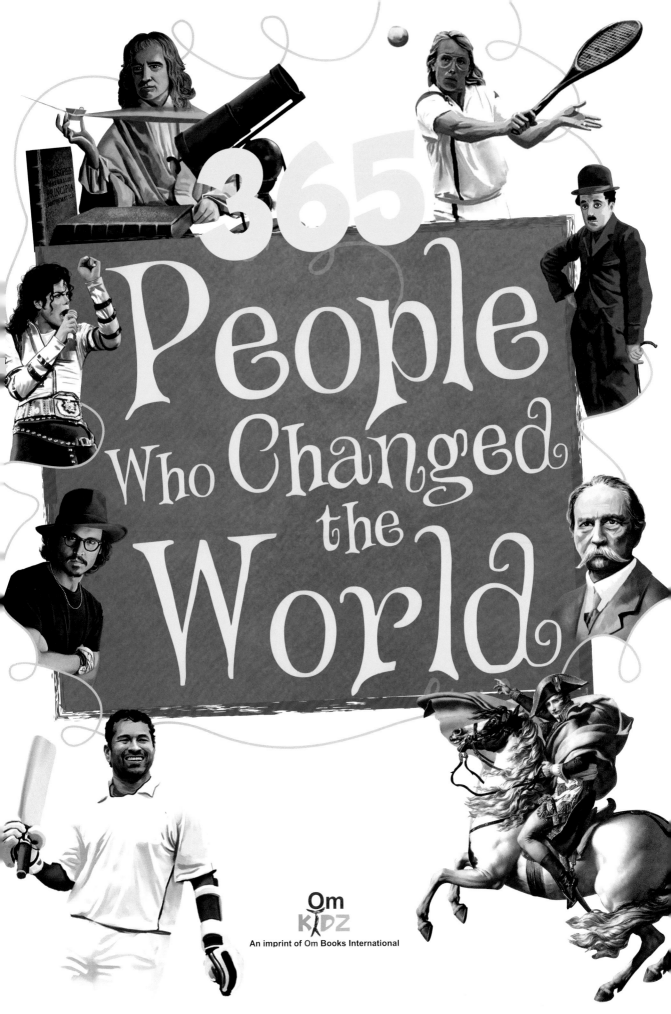

365
People
Who Changed
the
World

Om
KIDZ
An imprint of Om Books International

Contents

BUSINESS BOOMERS

GREATER GOOD

PHENOMENAL PHILOSOPHERS

LITERARY LORDS

AMAZING ARTISTS

MESMERISING MUSICIANS

FANTASTIC FOOD LORDS

FABULOUS FASHIONISTAS

Incredible Innovators

This section focusses on innovators whose work has contributed to important innovations. Let's find out about their inventions and contributions as well as their lives. Read on and get to know these incredible innovators better.

1. ALFRED NOBEL

Alfred Nobel was a Swedish chemist, engineer, entrepreneur and inventor with 354 patents to his name. He was born on 21st October, 1833, in Stockholm, Sweden. As a young man, he worked at his father's arms factory. While studying in Paris, he met Sobero, an Italian chemist, who invented nitro-glycerine, a highly explosive liquid. Nobel was interested in the use of nitro-glycerine for construction. While experimenting in 1866, he mixed it with a fine sand called "Kieselguhr" that turned the liquid into paste. He converted this paste into rods that could then be inserted into drilling holes. Nobel got a patent on this material and named it "dynamite."

His work and inventions made him a wealthy man. He used this fortune to establish the Nobel Prize, which honours people all around the world for their great accomplishments in physics, chemistry, medicine, literature and world peace. He died on 10th December, 1896.

2. NIKOLA TESLA

Nikola Tesla was a famous electrical engineer, futurist and inventor, who is best known for his design of the modern electrical supply system. He was born on 10th July, 1856, in modern day Croatia. Tesla studied in Austria and went to America to work with Thomas Edison.

Tesla's most renowned invention was the "Tesla coil" in 1891, which is still used in radio technology. Tesla was also a pioneer in the discovery of radar and X-ray technology. Though his patents earned him a lot of money, he spent a lot on experiments too. He died in poverty on 7th January, 1943, in New York.

3. MARCO POLO

Marco Polo was a well-known merchant and traveller. He was born in 1254 in Venice, Italy. He travelled throughout China as a messenger and spy for Kublai Khan of the Mongol Empire. During his trips all over Asia, he learned about different cultures, foods, cities and people. Marco told detailed stories of his journeys to a writer named Rustichello, who wrote them all down in a book called *The Travels of Marco Polo*.

He influenced European cartography, altering the world map with his discoveries. He passed away on 8th January, 1324, in Venice, Italy.

4. CHARLES GOODYEAR

Charles Goodyear was an American entrepreneur, who developed the process of vulcanisation of rubber. He was born on 29th December, 1800, in Connecticut, USA. In 1834, he went to a rubber company to sell a valve he had made and discovered that rubber melted to glue in hot weather. Goodyear then conducted many experiments with rubber, discovered the process of vulcanisation and patented it in 1844. This process made rubber water-proof and weather-proof, and revolutionised its use. Goodyear died on 1st July, 1860, in New York City. The Goodyear Tyre and Rubber Company was founded in his name in 1898 by Frank Seiberling.

5. JOHANNES GUTENBERG

Johannes Gutenberg was a German blacksmith, goldsmith, publisher and printer who is known as the "father of printing". He was born in 1398 in Mainz, Germany. He is best known for his invention of the modern printing press in 1439. This former stone cutter's masterpiece was the first book ever printed from a movable press. It was the *42–line Bible*, completed in 1455.

Gutenberg's printing press led to a dramatic increase in printing and started an interest in journalism. It led to the creation of newspapers, books, journals and magazines. He passed away on 3rd February, 1468, in Mainz, Germany.

6. NICOLAUS COPERNICUS

Nicolaus Copernicus was a Polish mathematician, scholar, economist, artist, diplomat and an astronomer. He was born on 19th February, 1473, in Torun, Poland. In 1496, he travelled to Italy to study law. Copernicus is best known for his theory called "De Revolutionibus Orbium Coelestium", meaning, "On the Revolutions of the Celestial Spheres".

Copernicus' theory was commonly known as "heliocentrism". It states that the Sun is at the centre of the universe, while Earth and all the other planets rotate around it in circular paths. It was Copernicus' theory that led to an astronomical revolution. His theory greatly influenced many great scientists including Galileo, Kepler, Descartes and Newton.

Copernicus came up with this theory between 1508 and 1514. He wrote this in a manuscript called the *Commentariolus* (Little Commentary). However, the final version of his theory was published in 1543, the year he died. He passed away on 24th May, 1543.

We know certain facts about Copernicus' early life. But a biography written by his ardent disciple, Georg Joachim Rheticus, is unfortunately lost.

7. VASCO DA GAMA

Vasco da Gama was a Portuguese navigator and explorer, who was famous for the discovery of the sea route from Europe to India via the Cape of Good Hope in Africa. He was born in Sines, Portugal, in 1460.

Vasco da Gama was given a fleet of ships by the King of Portugal to find a trade route around Africa to India. He left on his first voyage from Lisbon, Portugal, on 8th July, 1497, with 170 men and 4 ships. He returned home a hero, as he found the trade route to India. He passed away on 24th December, 1524, in Cochin, India.

8. LOUIS BRAILLE

Louis Braille was a French educator famous for inventing a system of reading, writing and printing, exclusively for the blind. He was born on 4th January, 1809, in Coupvray, near Paris, France. He was blinded in an accident when he was three years old. He attended the Royal Institute for Blind Youth, where he studied with raised imprints of letters on an embossed paper. He published his code in which he used six raised dots in different combinations in 1829. He also developed the Braille code for music. He died on 6th January, 1852.

9. ISAAC NEWTON

Sir Isaac Newton was an English physicist and mathematician, who is considered to be one of the most influential scientists of all time. He was born on 4th January, 1643, in Woolsthorpe, England. After finishing school in 1661, he went to Cambridge University, where he concentrated on science, mathematics and philosophy. He read books by Galileo, Rene Descartes, Euclid and Johannes Kepler. He became a professor soon after he graduated from Cambridge around 1669.

The discovery of the gravitational theory is credited to Isaac Newton. He is the one who found a relation between gravity and heavenly bodies in the solar system. He realised that the same relation exists between the Earth and the objects on it. After his discovery of the gravitational force, Newton elaborated on his theory, giving us the three laws of gravity. Gravity plays a large role in our daily lives and Newton's research has made it easier for us to understand this phenomenon. He died on 20th March, 1727, in London, England.

Newton published his legendary book, *Philosophiae Naturalis Principia Mathematica* in 1687, a masterpiece that introduced the world to the three laws of motion and the universal principle of gravity.

10. THOMAS NEWCOMEN

Thomas Newcomen was an English engineer and inventor, who invented the first steam engine. He was born on 24th February, 1664, in Dartmouth, England.

As Newcomen was an ironmonger by profession, he was aware that pumping water out of mines with the help of horses was very expensive. He conducted research for more than 10 years on inventing a steam pump. He made a significant contribution with his invention of the steam engine. His first working engine was installed at a coalmine at Dudley Castle in Staffordshire in 1712. Thomas Newcomen passed away on 5th August, 1729, in London, England.

11. BENJAMIN FRANKLIN

Benjamin Franklin was not only one of the founding fathers of the USA, but also a well-renowned printer, scientist, inventor, author, politician and diplomat. He was born on 17th January, 1706, in Boston. Even as a child, his passion for reading and experimentation was very intense. He wrote many letters and books.

He suspected that lightning was an electrical current and conducted an experiment to see if it would pass through metal. He invented the lighting rod, Franklin stove and bifocal glasses among other things. He conducted extensive research and published many theories about electricity. He died on 17th April, 1790.

12. JAMES WATT

James Watt was a Scottish inventor and mechanical engineer, renowned for his work on the steam engine. He was born on 30th January, 1736, in Greenock, Scotland. Watt designed a separate condensing chamber for the steam engine that immensely prevented the loss of power and steam. He received his first patent in 1769 for this device.

By 1790, Watt was an accomplished and wealthy man. He patented several other important inventions including the rotary engine, the double-action engine and the steam indicator. The unit of measurement of electrical and mechanical power, "Watt", is named in his honour. Watt died on 25th August, 1819, in Heathfield, Scotland.

13. CHARLES BABBAGE

Charles Babbage was an English inventor and mathematician, who is also known as the "father of computers". He was born in London on 26th December, 1791. He was often unwell as a child and was educated mainly at home. He later grew fond of mathematics and went on to pursue it further at Cambridge University in 1810. In 1820, he invented the "difference engine", a machine which could perform mathematical calculations. His mathematical machines were based on ideas that were later used in modern computers. He passed away at his home in London on 18th October, 1871.

14. GALILEO GALILEI

Galileo Galilei was an Italian mathematician, astronomer, physicist and philosopher. He was born on 15th February, 1564, in Pisa, Italy. He grew up during the Italian Renaissance, which greatly influenced him. Galileo began his education at the Camaldolese monastery. He was an accomplished musician and an excellent student. He went to the University of Pisa to study medicine in 1581, but he soon became interested in physics and mathematics.

Galileo experimented with pendulums, levers, balls and other objects. He tried to describe how they moved with mathematic equations. His experimentation led to the invention of the advanced measuring device called the "hydrostatic balance". In 1609, having heard of the invention of a telescope, he decided to build his own telescope. He took the archaic telescope and made great improvements to it. Galileo used it extensively to observe outer space. Soon, Galileo's advanced version of the telescope was used throughout Europe. He passed away in Arcetri on 8th January, 1642.

Galileo made many discoveries using the telescope, such as the four large moons around Jupiter and the phases of the planet Venus. He also discovered sunspots and stated that the Moon was not smooth and was, in fact, covered with craters.

15. CHARLES DARWIN

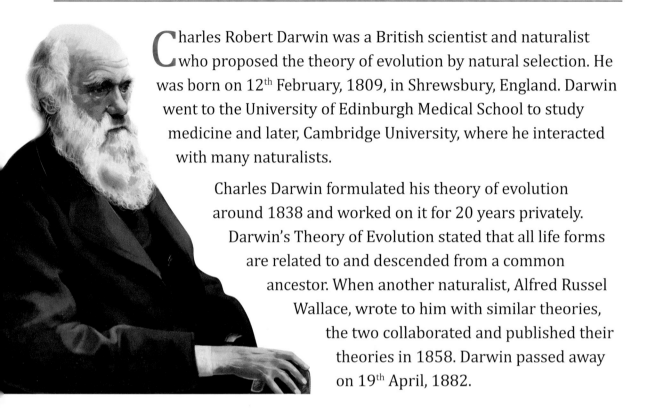

Charles Robert Darwin was a British scientist and naturalist who proposed the theory of evolution by natural selection. He was born on 12th February, 1809, in Shrewsbury, England. Darwin went to the University of Edinburgh Medical School to study medicine and later, Cambridge University, where he interacted with many naturalists.

Charles Darwin formulated his theory of evolution around 1838 and worked on it for 20 years privately. Darwin's Theory of Evolution stated that all life forms are related to and descended from a common ancestor. When another naturalist, Alfred Russel Wallace, wrote to him with similar theories, the two collaborated and published their theories in 1858. Darwin passed away on 19th April, 1882.

16. SAMUEL COLT

Samuel Colt was an American inventor and industrialist who was famous for his invention of the revolver and its mass production for commercial sale. He was born on 19th July, 1814, in Hartford, Connecticut, USA. He studied in Glastonbury and started working at his father's mill at the age of 15.

Colt made a wooden model of the revolver when he was young and patented it in France, England and USA. His invention made him a rich man. He died on 10th January, 1862.

17. ERATOSTHENES OF CYRENE

Eratosthenes was a famous Greek scientific scholar, mathematician, geologist, geographer and astronomer. He was the first person to use the word "geography" in Greek and invented the subject of geography as defined today. Eratosthenes was born around 276 BCE in Cyrene (modern day Libya).

Eratosthenes' initial years were spent in Cyrene, but later he went to Athens for further studies. He proposed a simple algorithm for finding prime numbers. He was also the first person to make a map including parallels and meridians, which is now known as latitudes and longitudes. He was also the first person to give a relatively accurate measurement of the Earth's circumference.

He rightly deduced that as the Sun is at a great distance from the Earth, the rays are almost parallel when they hit the Earth. Using this knowledge and the distance between two cities, he was able to roughly measure the Earth's circumference!

His mathematical work was highlighted in the writings of Greek geometer Pappus of Alexandria. His geographical work was brought to light in the books of Greek geographer Strabo. Eratosthenes passed away in 194 BCE at the age of 82.

18. KARL BENZ

Karl Benz was a German car engineer who invented the petrol-powered car. He was born on 25th November, 1844, in Muhlburg, Germany. In spite of being poor, his mother gave him the best education that his family could afford. Benz studied at the local grammar school in Karlsruhe. He completed his higher studies at the Polytechnical University under the instruction of Ferdinand Redtenbacher. He was originally interested in locksmithing, but eventually followed his father's footsteps towards locomotive engineering. During these years, he dreamed of inventing a vehicle that would eventually become a "horseless carriage".

In 1885, Benz built a gasoline-powered car. This automobile, known as the motor car, remained a rare invention for which he got his first patent. Though there were other people in Germany working on a similar invention, Karl Benz got the patent first. He soon started his own company called "Benz and Company". It became the world's largest manufacturer of automobiles by 1900. He passed away on 4th April, 1929.

The original Benz car had only three wheels and was called the "Motorwagen". It is currently preserved in Munich. It first ran in early 1885, but its design was not patented until 29th January, 1886.

19. THOMAS EDISON

Thomas Alva Edison was a scientist and inventor, who pioneered several significant inventions. He was born on 11th February, 1847, in Ohio, USA. Edison began working at the young age of 13. By the age of 16, he was working as a telegraph operator. He soon became interested in communications, which was the focus of many of his inventions.

Edison is most well-known for inventing the phonograph, the electric light bulb and the motion picture. He invented ways of producing electricity and distributing it through wires. Edison power stations were all over the world by the 1890s. He passed away on 18th October, 1931, in West Orange, New Jersey.

20. ALEXANDER GRAHAM BELL

Alexander Graham Bell was an influential scientist, engineer and inventor. He was born on 3rd March, 1847, in Edinburgh, Scotland. He is widely credited with the invention of the first practical telephone. His mother and wife were both deaf, which had a major influence on his work. He also had a strong interest in other scientific fields such as developing the photophone, conducting medical research and searching for alternative fuel sources. He passed away on 2nd August, 1922.

21. ARYABHATA

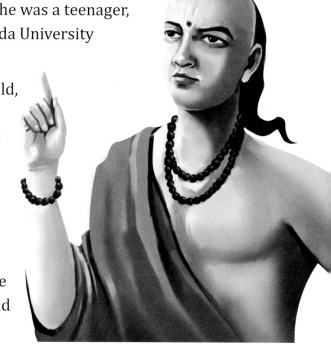

Aryabhata was one of India's greatest mathematicians. He was born around 476 CE. When he was a teenager, he left his hometown and went to Nalanda University in Kusumapura.

By the time Aryabhata was 23 years old, he was already writing his first book, known as *Aryabhatiya*, which was about math and astronomy. He was one of the first to state that the Earth spins on its axis. He also calculated the value of pi to be 3.1416, which is very close to the actual value—3.14159. But his greatest contribution to mathematics remains the "zero", without which mathematics would not be the same. He died in 550 CE.

22. RUDOLF DIESEL

Rudolph Christian Karl Diesel was a German inventor and engineer, who invented the famous internal combustion engine commonly known as the diesel engine.

He was born on 18th March, 1858, in Paris, France. Although Diesel's parents were German, the family lived in Paris till 1870. Diesel studied at the Technical High School in Munich and excelled at engineering. He thought of making an internal combustion engine and conceived the idea in about 1890. He patented it in 1892 and it became a huge success. He died on 29th September, 1913.

23. LEO HENDRIK BAEKELAND

Leo Hendrik Baekeland was an American chemist best known for his invention of Bakelite. He was born on 14th November, 1863, in Ghent, Belgium. Baekeland received his doctorate from the University of Ghent at the age of 21 and taught there until 1889.

He soon set up his own company to manufacture his first invention "Velox", a photographic printing paper, which could be developed under artificial light. He then started his own laboratory in New York, where he invented Bakelite in 1907. It was the first synthetic plastic which opened doors to the use of plastic in the future. He passed away on 23rd February, 1944.

24. THE WRIGHT BROTHERS

Brothers Wilbur and Orville Wright were inventors and pioneers in the aviation industry. Wilbur was born in Millville, Indiana, on 16th April, 1867, and Orville was born in Dayton, Ohio, on 19th August, 1871. They went to high school but did not get their diplomas. On 17th December, 1903, the Wright brothers launched the first successful air flight in Kitty Hawk.

They were the first to make a successful aircraft that was powered by an engine. They received a patent for their design in 1906.

25. GUGLIELMO MARCONI

Guglielmo Marconi was a physicist and inventor, who was best known for his work on radio transmission. He was born on 25th April, 1874, in Bologna, Italy. Marconi began experimenting with electro-magnetics as a student at the Livorno Technical Institute. He developed a system of wireless telegraphy for which he received his first patent in England.

He was awarded the Nobel Prize in Physics with Karl Ferdinand Braun for their development of practical wireless telegraphy. His development of a radio telegraph system led to the establishment of many associated wireless inventions. He died in Rome on 20th July, 1937.

26. LEE DE FOREST

Lee De Forest was an American inventor who is remembered as the "father of the radio" and the "grandfather of the television". He was born on 26th August, 1873, in Iowa, USA. Even as a child, he was fascinated with machinery and technological advancements.

He experimented with long-distance radio signals and, in 1906, invented an electronic device named the "audion vacuum tube". His invention laid the foundation for the field of electronics. He passed away on 30th June, 1961, in Hollywood, California.

27. ALBERT EINSTEIN

German genius, Albert Einstein, was born on 14th March, 1879, in Ulm, Germany. He had exceptional grades in physics and mathematics. Two things sparked his interest in the sciences. One was a compass that his father gave him when he was 10 years old. The other was a geometry book he found when he was 12. Soon after he graduated, Einstein worked in a patent office evaluating patents for electromagnetic devices.

He worked on many influential theories and projects. Einstein came up with theories about light, matter, gravity, space and time. Einstein is more than just a world-famous scientist, his name represents intelligence and knowledge! In 1921, he received the Nobel Prize for his achievements in theoretical physics. He is best known for developing the theory of relativity. He is regarded as one of the most brilliant minds of the 20th century. He died on 18th April, 1955.

Einstein didn't do very well in school and one teacher even told him that he would never be successful.

28. ALEXANDER FLEMING

Alexander Fleming was a world famous pharmacologist and botanist. He was born on 6th August, 1881. His most popular discoveries are the enzyme lysozyme in 1921 and penicillin, the antibiotic, in 1928. He originally wanted to become a surgeon, but after spending time in the laboratories of the Inoculation Department at St. Mary's Hospital, he decided to pursue bacteriology instead. During World War I, he worked as a bacteriologist with the Royal Army Medical Corps and studied soldiers' wounds. He discovered that using strong antiseptics on wounds actually did more harm than good.

In 1928, Fleming made an accidental discovery from a contaminated petri dish. The contaminated bacteria contained a powerful antibiotic, which was later called penicillin. Penicillin stops the growth of harmful bacteria that is responsible for many other dangerous diseases. He, along with two other scientists, received a Nobel Prize for his discovery in 1945. Fleming saved millions of lives with his accidental discovery! He passed away on 11th March, 1955.

His discovery of lysozyme was also accidental. He was studying a culture plate of bacteria when a bit of his mucus fell in it. A few days later, he saw signs of the bacteria dissolving.

29. PERCY LEBARON SPENCER

Percy Lebaron Spencer was an American engineer and inventor, who is famous for the invention of the microwave oven. He was born on 19th July, 1894, in Howland, Maine, USA. Spencer went to school for a brief period before starting work at the age of 12. Spencer learnt in detail about electricity when he was 16 years old. He also taught himself chemistry, physics, trigonometry and calculus.

While working with Raytheon, a US defence contractor, he accidently discovered how a candy bar had melted while working near a radar set. This led to the invention of the microwave oven. He died on 8th September, 1970.

30. PHILO FARNSWORTH

Philo Taylor Farnsworth was an American scientist and inventor. He was born on 19th August, 1906, in Utah, USA. This talented prodigy began inventing gadgets in grade school.

In 1938, Farnsworth unveiled a prototype of the first all-electric television that he had sketched in his chemistry class as a teenager. He led the research in nuclear fusion. Farnsworth also contributed to the development of the baby incubator, the electron microscope, the astronomical telescope and infra red night vision devices. He passed away on 11th March, 1971, in Salt Lake City, USA.

31. ROBERT NOYCE

Robert Norton Noyce is also known as the "Mayor of Silicon Valley" as he was the co-inventor of the microchip that led to the personal computer revolution. He was born on 12th December, 1927, in Burlington, Iowa. He grew up in Grinnel, Iowa and completed his studies there.

Noyce ran two of the companies that had the greatest impact on the silicon industry—"Fairchild Semiconductor" and "Intel". When he was at Intel, Noyce managed and looked after Ted Hoff's invention of the microprocessor. He passed away on 3rd June, 1990, in Austin, Texas.

32. MARTIN COOPER

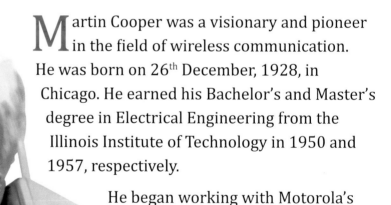

Martin Cooper was a visionary and pioneer in the field of wireless communication. He was born on 26th December, 1928, in Chicago. He earned his Bachelor's and Master's degree in Electrical Engineering from the Illinois Institute of Technology in 1950 and 1957, respectively.

He began working with Motorola's Cellular Research project. He invented the first wireless cellular phone in 1973. It took about 17 years from the first phone call for cellular communication to be fully developed and marketed to the world.

33. STEPHEN HAWKING

Stephen William Hawking is an English physicist, cosmologist and author. He was born on 8th January, 1942, in Oxford, England. He completed his schooling in England and went to Oxford University for higher studies.

He moved to Cambridge University to carry out research in Cosmology. When he returned home after his first term at Cambridge, he experienced clumsiness and a slight speech impediment. Shortly after his 21st birthday, he was diagnosed with an incurable form of a motor neurone disease. Doctors initially gave Hawking two years to live. He began using a wheelchair and eventually lost his power of speech.

He is most well-known for his contribution on the "Big Bang Theory" and the discovery of "Black Holes". He completed his PhD and enjoys a career as a leading theoretical physicist. In 1979, he was appointed as the Lucasian Professor of Mathematics at Cambridge, the most famous academic chair in the world.

In 1974, Hawking was inducted into the Royal Society, a worldwide fellowship of scientists. He was awarded the Eddington Medal from the Royal Astronomical Society. He prides himself for making his complex physical concepts accessible to the common public by writing the bestseller, *A Brief History of Time.*

34. TIM BERNERS-LEE

S ir Timothy John "Tim" Berners-Lee is a British computer scientist known for the invention of the world wide web. He was born on 8th June, 1955, in London, England. He went to Queen's College, Oxford University, where he received a degree in physics.

In 1990, he produced the first version of the world wide web, the first web browser and the first web server. It was available online in 1991. He is currently the Director of the World Wide Web Consortium, the group that oversees the standards of the web.

35. SID MEIER

S id Meier is a Canadian-American programmer and designer who is known as "the father of computer gaming". He was born on 24th February, 1954, in Detroit, USA. Meier graduated with a degree in computer science from the University of Michigan. In 1982, Sid co-founded "MicroProse Software" that made the first simulation video game—F 15 Strike Eagle.

Meier was inducted into the Academy of Interactive Arts and Science's Hall of Fame and the Computer Museum of America's Hall of Fame in 1999 and 2002, respectively. Meier and his games have been awarded with every major award in the gaming industry.

Legendary Leaders

There are some people who have shaped history and consequently the present. Some of them were revolutionary in the way they led their nation, some were great leaders for different reasons and some were just downright evil in their outlook. But their influence and leadership cannot be denied. Read on to find out more about these legendary leaders.

36. MAHATMA GANDHI

Mohandas Karamchand Gandhi was the most famous freedom fighter of the Indian nationalist movement against the British. He was born on 2nd October, 1869, in Porbander, Gujarat, India. He is fondly remembered as Gandhiji or Mahatma Gandhi. He studied law in England and took up a job as a lawyer in South Africa.

On his return to India, he followed non-violent methods of protests like fasts and marches against the British rule. The "Quit India Movement" initiated by him was a great success and India became independent on 15th August, 1947. He is fondly remembered as "Bapu" and "Father of the Nation" in India. He was assassinated on 30th January, 1948.

37. CYRUS THE GREAT

Cyrus the Great was a significant figure in the history of the Persian Empire. He was the first world leader to be referred to as "The Great". He was born around 590–580 BCE. Cyrus founded Persia by uniting the two original Iranian tribes—the Medes and the Persians.

Until he became king, Persia was a peaceful state of the Medes Empire. Under his rule, the Persian Empire embraced the ancient Near East, most of Southwest Asia and much of Central Asia as well. Cyrus declared the first Charter of Human Rights known to humankind. He passed away in about 530 BCE.

38. ALEXANDER THE GREAT

Prince Alexander III of Macedonia is known as Alexander the Great. He was born on 20ᵗʰ July, 356 BCE, in Pella, Macedonia. He was educated by the famous philosopher Aristotle.

He set out to conquer the massive Persian Empire. Against overwhelming odds, he led his army to victories across the Persian territories of Asia, Syria and Egypt, without suffering a single defeat. He founded more than 70 cities throughout the Mediterranean region and west up to India, spreading trade and the Greek culture wherever he went. He passed away at the young age of 32 in 324 BCE.

39. ASHOKA

King Ashoka was an Indian emperor of the Mauryan Dynasty, who ruled most of the Indian sub-continent during his reign. Born in 304 BCE, he ascended the throne by 273 BCE. Ashoka was a great philanthropist and worked for the welfare of his people.

He converted to Buddhism after the famous Kalinga War and ceased all military conquest and violence. He built many monuments in Buddha's honour. To honour Ashoka's achievements, the Government of India has adopted the Ashoka Chakra on the Sarnath Pillar built during his reign as the country's national symbol. He died in 232 BCE.

40. QIN SHI HUANG

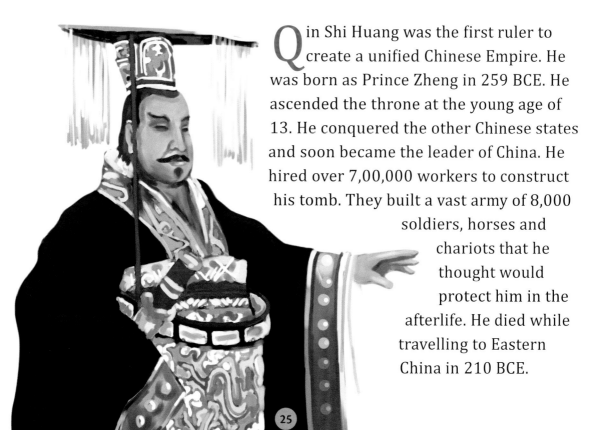

Qin Shi Huang was the first ruler to create a unified Chinese Empire. He was born as Prince Zheng in 259 BCE. He ascended the throne at the young age of 13. He conquered the other Chinese states and soon became the leader of China. He hired over 7,00,000 workers to construct his tomb. They built a vast army of 8,000 soldiers, horses and chariots that he thought would protect him in the afterlife. He died while travelling to Eastern China in 210 BCE.

41. JULIUS CAESAR

Julius Caesar was a famous Roman general, statesman and author. He was born in Rome around 100 BCE to an aristocratic family. He became the head of his family at the young age of 16 after his father passed away. Julius Caesar joined the Roman Army in 81 BCE and was the first Roman to invade England in 55 BCE and again in 54 BCE.

In 65 BCE, Caesar was appointed an "adele", which put him in charge of Rome's public entertainment. He became very popular amongst the Romans. Soon after, Caesar joined the army and left Rome in order to avoid Sulla, the dictator of Rome and his allies.

When Sulla died, Caesar returned to Rome in about 46 BCE. He was a military hero from his years in the army and he quickly rose up the ranks of the Roman government. He made significant changes to Rome by constructing new buildings and temples. He soon became the most powerful man in Europe as the Senate made him the dictator. He was assassinated on 15th March, 44 BCE.

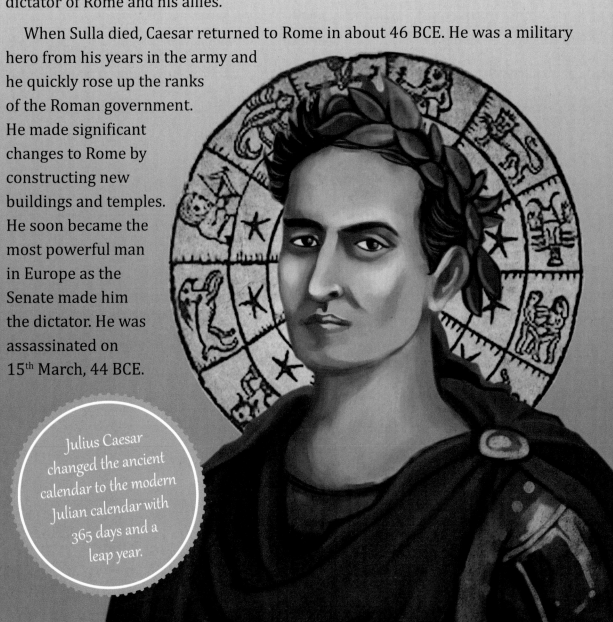

Julius Caesar changed the ancient calendar to the modern Julian calendar with 365 days and a leap year.

42. CONSTANTINE

Constantine the Great is one of history's most popular leaders. He was born in 272 CE in modern Serbia. He was well-educated.

He was the first Roman emperor to follow Christianity. He laid the foundation for the growth of western medieval culture. He ruled from 306–337 CE. While he ruled the Eastern Roman Empire, he chose his capital to be the small town of Byzantium, which he renamed Constantinople. Constantinople remained the seat of the Eastern Roman Empire until 1453. He passed away in 337 CE.

43. NERO

Nero Claudius Caesar Augustus Germanicus, also known as Nero, was the fifth Roman emperor, who was infamous for the alleged burning of Rome to construct his famous landscape villa known as the Domus Aurea or the "Golden House". He was born on 15th December, 37 CE.

Nero succeeded the throne in 54 CE, following Claudius' death. He was

popular amongst the people as he eliminated capital punishment and allowed slaves to bring complaints against their masters. Nero was described as a generous and reasonable leader until he got his mother murdered in the year 59 CE. He passed away on 9th June, 68 CE, in Rome.

44. WILLIAM THE CONQUEROR

William the Conqueror, or William I, was one of the greatest rulers of England. He was born around 1028 in Normandy, France. William I was crowned Duke of Normandy in 1035, when he was just seven years old.

Not only did he conquer England, he also made it the most powerful government in Europe. William I popularised the English language. Although he never spoke English and was illiterate, he significantly influenced the evolution of the English language. He added many French and Latin words to the English dictionary. William ruled England until his death on 9th September, 1087, in Rouen, France.

45. SALADIN

Saladin was the first Sultan of Egypt and Syria who founded the famous Ayyubid dynasty. He was born around 1138 Tikrit, Mesopotamia, which is now in Iraq.

He gained control over Yemen and Palestine as well. He was a strict and ruthless ruler. He had tremendous military and political skills to remain the unquestioned leader of the Arabs. He encouraged the growth and spread of Islamic religious institutions. He courted their scholars and preachers as well as constructed colleges and mosques. He passed away in 1193.

46. GENGHIS KHAN

Genghis Khan was one of the most famous conquerors of history, who founded the Mongolian Empire. He was born in Mongolia around 1162. His father was the chief of his tribe, but was killed when Genghis was quite young. The tribe, refusing to be led by someone so young, forced him and his family to go into exile. Slowly, he started making alliances with different tribes and at the young age of 20, he successfully built a large army. He subdued various tribes of Northeast Asia under his rule. At the age of 27, he was elected Khan.

After uniting the nomadic tribes of Mongolia, he conquered most of central Asia and China. At their peak, the Mongols controlled an area almost the size of Africa. Many historians have written about the Mongol invasions and the destruction they caused. The Mongol Empire was the largest empire in the world before the British Empire and lasted much after Genghis Khan's death in 1227.

During his years in exile with his mother and brothers, they were forced to live on wild fruits, ox carcasses and small game that they could hunt.

47. LORENZO DE' MEDICI

Lorenzo de' Medici or "Lorenzo the Magnificent" was an Italian statesman and Florentine's famous ruler and patron during the Italian Renaissance. He was born on 1st January, 1449, in Florence. Italy. He ruled Florence initially with his brother, Giuliano, and on his own after his brother's assassination. He was best known for his patronage of the arts. Those under his protection included great Renaissance artists such as Botticelli and Leonardo da Vinci. He passed away on 9th April, 1492.

48. JOAN OF ARC

Joan d'Arc also known as "Joan of Arc" or the "Maid of Orleans" was a Roman Catholic saint who believed she was working under divine guidance. She was born around 1412 in Domrémy, France. She was a peasant girl who had mystical visions about her leadership in a battle between the French and the English.

Joan of Arc was captured during battle at the city of Compiegne. She was executed by the English at the young age of 19 on 30th May, 1431.

49. HENRY VIII

Henry VIII was the King of England. He presided over the initial stages of the English Renaissance and the English Reformation. He was born on 28th June, 1491, in England. He excelled at book learning and physical activity as a child.

He was appointed Duke of York and Lord Lieutenant of Ireland while he was still a child. In 1501, he was appointed as the Prince of Wales. In 1509, when Henry was 18 years old, he succeeded the throne after his father's death. He died at the age of 56 in 1547.

50. SULEIMAN THE MAGNIFICENT

Suleiman I or Suleiman the Magnificent was the longest reigning Sultan of the Ottoman Empire. He was born on 6th November, 1494, in Trabzon, Turkey. Suleiman I wanted to be a governor when he was 15 years old. After Selim I passed away, he succeeded the throne.

Suleiman I prepared written laws and applied them strictly. He was often called "Kanuni" or Law Giver. He reined for 46 years from 1520 to 1566. He led his empire to prosperity which was never surpassed. He died on 7th September, 1566, while he was commanding the siege of Sziget.

51. QUEEN ELIZABETH I

Queen Elizabeth I, also known as "Gloriana" or "Good Queen Bess", was the fifth and last monarch of the Tudor Dynasty of England. She was born on 7th September, 1533, in Greenwich, England. She was crowned Queen of England on 15th January, 1559.

Highly educated, Elizabeth I turned her court into a centre for learning.

She also strengthened the currency and promoted government reforms, leading to a growth of the economy. Elizabeth's 45-year reign is known as the Elizabethan Age, during which England became a strong European power. She died on 24th March, 1603, in Richmond, England.

52. PETER THE GREAT

Peter the Great, or Peter I, was the ruler of the Tsar kingdom of Russia and later, the Russian Empire. He was born on 9th June, 1672, in Moscow.

He started the Northern War with Sweden in 1700 that lasted for 21 years and resulted in Russia's victory. When the Northern War ended, Russia was declared an empire and Peter the Great proclaimed himself as Emperor in 1721.

He was the first leader to organise a Russian army. He also founded the Russian navy. He passed away on 8th February, 1725.

53. GEORGE WASHINGTON

George Washington was the commander-in-chief of the colonial armies of the American Revolution, who went on to become the first President of the USA. He was born on 22ⁿᵈ February, 1732, in Virginia, USA. Washington grew up in Colonial Virginia. His father was a landowner and planter who died when Washington was just 11 years old. Washington first worked as a surveyor, which made him travel from one place to another for two years. He joined the colonial army in 1752 and went on to lead the colonial armies during the American Revolution.

Washington is known as one of the Founding Fathers of the USA. He was elected President in 1789 and served two terms in office. Washington also presided over the convention that drafted the United States Constitution. He went on a tour of the entire country to know the problems of the people and to find their solution. He passed away on 14ᵗʰ December, 1799, in Virginia.

George Washington gave the idea for greeting American presidents as "Mr. President". He is believed to have written 20,000 letters in his two terms as President.

54. THOMAS JEFFERSON

Thomas Jefferson was one of the Founding Fathers of the USA. He is most famous for being the main author of the Declaration of Independence. He was born on 13th April, 1743, in Shadwell, Virginia. Jefferson was believed to be an obsessive student, who spent more than 15 hours with his books on a regular basis.

In 1775, Jefferson was elected to the Continental Congress to write the Declaration of Independence which states that "all men are created equal". The declaration also states the reasons the colonists wanted to separate from England. He passed away on 4th July, 1826.

55. KING LOUIS XVI

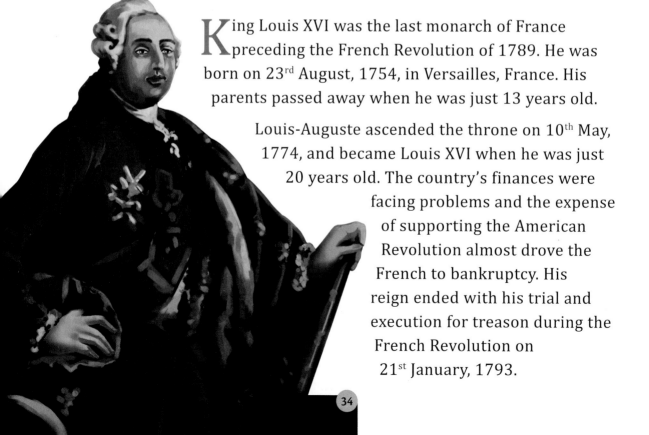

King Louis XVI was the last monarch of France preceding the French Revolution of 1789. He was born on 23rd August, 1754, in Versailles, France. His parents passed away when he was just 13 years old.

Louis-Auguste ascended the throne on 10th May, 1774, and became Louis XVI when he was just 20 years old. The country's finances were facing problems and the expense of supporting the American Revolution almost drove the French to bankruptcy. His reign ended with his trial and execution for treason during the French Revolution on 21st January, 1793.

56. NAPOLEON BONAPARTE

Napoleon Bonaparte was the first Consul and Emperor of France. He was born on 15th August, 1769, in Ajaccio, St. Helena Island. He received his education at a military school. He was promoted quite rapidly to the position of the Commander of the French army in the fight against Austria and its allies.

Napoleon defeated the British at Toulon and regained the territory for France. This made him popular and he also earned a promotion. Napoleon conquered Ottoman-ruled Egypt in 1798 to strike at British trade routes with India. He overthrew the French government and took control in 1799. He died on 5th May, 1821.

57. SIMÓN BOLÍVAR

Simón Bolívar was a South American soldier, who was the leader of the revolution against the Spanish Empire. He was born on 24th July, 1783, in Caracas, Venezuela. Initially, he was tutored at home and later completed his graduation in Europe.

Bolívar played an important role in the fight for independence against France. He joined the resistance movement when Napoleon named Joseph Bonaparte King of Spain. He succeeded in uniting most of South America in a federation free from Spanish control. He passed away on 17th December, 1830.

58. OTTO VON BISMARCK

Otto Eduard Leopold Von Bismarck was the founder and chancellor of the first German Empire. He was born on 1st April, 1815, in Schönhausen, Germany. At the age of 24, he decided to run his family's estate at Kneiphof. In 1847, he was sent to Berlin as a delegate to the new Prussian parliament, where he emerged as a reactionary voice against the liberal, anti-autocratic revolutions of 1848. He passed away on 30th July, 1898 in Friedrichsruh, Germany.

59. ABRAHAM LINCOLN

Abraham Lincoln was one of the most influential American presidents, who also abolished slavery. He was born on 12th February, 1809, in Kentucky, USA. He had very little formal schooling and educated himself to be a lawyer.

He was the 16th President of the USA. He successfully led his country through its worst constitutional and moral crisis—the American Civil War. In 1863, he issued the law and proclaimed the freedom of slaves in the Southern states. Gradually, slavery was banned all over America and all slaves were freed. He was assassinated in 1865 in Washington DC.

60. VLADIMIR LENIN

Vladimir Illych Ulyanov was a politician and a Russian communist, who was the first head of the Soviet State. He was born on 22ⁿᵈ April, 1870, in Ulyanovsk, Russia. He was an excellent student. He joined the revolutionary movement and changed his name to Lenin to avoid arrest.

Lenin spent the years leading up to the 1917 Revolution in exile. He was the founder of the Russian Communist Party. He established the first communist government in 1917. He died in 1924.

61. QUEEN VICTORIA

Alexandrina Victoria, famously known as Queen Victoria, was the longest reigning monarch in English history. She was born on 24ᵗʰ May, 1819, in London, England. She was just 18 when she ascended the throne. After the death of her husband, Prince Albert, she went through a phase of depression, staying out of public view for three years. When Queen Victoria recovered, she began to take a strong interest in the British Empire and its colonies. Queen Victoria's 63-year long, victorious reign was known as the Victorian Age. She died on 22ⁿᵈ January, 1901.

62. KING KHUFU

Khnum-Khufu was an Egyptian pharaoh well-known for the construction of one of the Seven Wonders of the World—the Great Pyramid of Giza. He ascended the throne in 2589 BCE.

He came to power when he was just 20 years old and started working on his pyramid immediately. It took him about 23 years to complete the entire project. A total of 23,00,000 building blocks were moved, each one weighing about 2.5 tons! To create a monument of this magnitude in those days is phenomenal and historians are still speculating how it was built. Some historians claim that he used slaves, others believe that they were paid labourers.

The surviving depiction of King Khufu is the smallest piece of Egyptian royal sculpture ever discovered – 3-inch-tall tall ivory statue. It is estimated that his reign ended with his death in 2566 BCE.

63. THEODORE ROOSEVELT

Theodore Roosevelt was a soldier and a writer who became the 26th President of the USA. He was born on 27th October, 1858, in New York. He was educated by private tutors and was a very intelligent child.

When the Spanish War broke out in 1898, he formed a voluntary group of soldiers who called themselves "Rough Riders". They became famous after their victorious fight in Cuba. He served as the American President from 1901–1909. He worked hard to improve the quality of life for the average American. He died on 6th January, 1919.

64. SIR WINSTON CHURCHILL

Sir Winston Churchill was a British author, statesman and politician who served as Britain's Prime Minister during World War II. He was born on 30th November, 1874, in Oxfordshire, England. Churchill had a poor academic record due to which his father made him join the army. He became popular as a journalist while he reported his travels to Spain during the Cuban War of Independence and his visit to British India.

In 1900, Churchill won a seat to the British Parliament and became the Prime Minister in 1940. His leadership during World War II enabled the British Empire to stand against Hitler and the Germans. Churchill led Britain from the brink of defeat to victory. He served his country for many years. Churchill authored many books, some of which are *History of the English-Speaking Peoples*, *The Second World War*, *Savrola* and *The River War*. Churchill was also awarded the Nobel Prize for Literature for his work, especially *The Second World War*. Churchill resigned from active politics in 1955. He died on 24th January, 1965.

Sir Winston Churchill was an amateur painter who painted more than 600 paintings in his lifetime.

65. MUHAMMAD ALI JINNAH

Muhammad Ali Jinnah was an Indian politician, who was the first governor-general and founder of Pakistan. Jinnah was born on 25th December, 1876, in Karachi, Pakistan. He completed his matriculation from University of Bombay and went to England to study law.

Jinnah joined the Indian National Congress in 1906. He joined the Muslim League seven years later. The independent state of Pakistan as envisioned by Jinnah became a reality on 14th August, 1947. He was sworn in as Pakistan's first governor-general the next day. He is famous in Pakistan as "Quaid-I Azam" or "Great Leader". On 11th September, 1948, he died near Karachi, Pakistan.

66. JOSEPH STALIN

Joseph Stalin was one of the most powerful dictators of the Soviet Union, who transformed it into a major world power. He was born on 18th December, 1878, in Georgia. His reign of terror caused the suffering and death of millions, but he played a key role in the defeat of Nazism.

Stalin promoted himself as Lenin's heir when the latter died in 1924. Later, he defeated all his rivals and became the dictator of the Soviet Union by the late 1920s. He died on 5th March, 1953.

67. FRANKLIN ROOSEVELT

Franklin D. Roosevelt was the 32ⁿᵈ President of America and the only one to be elected to office four times. He was born on 30ᵗʰ January, 1882, in New York. His father pushed him to study law at Columbia University Law School, but he had little interest for the legal profession.

Roosevelt was elected to the New York Senate, where he rose as a Democratic politician. He led his country through two of the greatest crises of the 20ᵗʰ century—the Great Depression and World War II. He died on 12ᵗʰ April, 1945, in Warm Springs, Georgia.

68. BENITO MUSSOLINI

Benito Mussolini was an Italian journalist, politician and fascist dictator. He was born in 1883 in Forli, Italy. His father influenced a passion for socialist politics and defiance against authority in him. Mussolini followed in his father's political footsteps, but was expelled by his party for his support of World War I.

In 1919, Mussolini created the Fascist Party. He was elected as Prime Minister in 1922. He ruled constitutionally till 1925, after which he assumed dictatorship and gained all the power in Italy. He was one of the key figures in the creation of fascism.

He exploited his forces during World War II and was killed by his own people on 28ᵗʰ April, 1945, in Mezzegra, Italy.

69. ADOLF HITLER

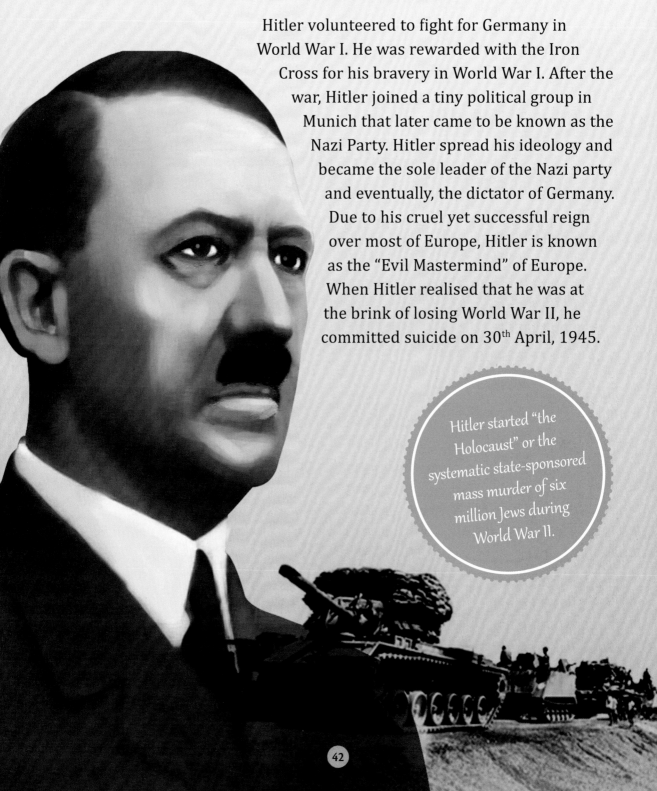

Adolf Hitler was the leader of the Nazi party and one of the most powerful dictators of all times. His aggressive actions are considered to be one of the causes of World War II. He was born on 20th April, 1889, in Austria. Hitler did not do well in school and wanted to become an artist.

Hitler volunteered to fight for Germany in World War I. He was rewarded with the Iron Cross for his bravery in World War I. After the war, Hitler joined a tiny political group in Munich that later came to be known as the Nazi Party. Hitler spread his ideology and became the sole leader of the Nazi party and eventually, the dictator of Germany. Due to his cruel yet successful reign over most of Europe, Hitler is known as the "Evil Mastermind" of Europe. When Hitler realised that he was at the brink of losing World War II, he committed suicide on 30th April, 1945.

Hitler started "the Holocaust" or the systematic state-sponsored mass murder of six million Jews during World War II.

70. JAWAHARLAL NEHRU

Jawaharlal Nehru was the first Prime Minister of India. He was born on 14th November, 1889, in Allahabad, India. Initially, Nehru was educated at home. Later, he studied at Trinity College, Cambridge.

Nehru was interested in politics. He went on to become Mahatma Gandhi's favourite disciple and an important leader in the Indian freedom struggle. Jawaharlal Nehru, also referred to as "Pandit Nehru", is considered to be one of the architects of modern India. Nehru was affectionately referred to as Chacha Nehru as he was very fond of children. He died on 27th May, 1964.

71. CHARLES DE GAULLE

Charles de Gaulle was a French soldier, writer and statesman, who is often known as the Father of France. He was born on 22nd November, 1890, in Lille, France. He came from a family of writers, teachers and administrators. However, he decided to join the army. He was the leader of the Free French Forces that fought during World War II. He founded the French Fifth Republic and became its first president. He guided France through the writing of the constitution. He passed away on 9th November, 1970.

72. JOSEPH MCCARTHY

Joseph McCarthy was a famous American politician, who served as a US senator from 1947 to 1957. He was born on 14th November, 1908, in Wisconsin, USA. McCarthy studied law from Marquette University. The term "McCarthyism" was developed to refer to McCarthy's anti-communist practices.

McCarthy was an attorney. He served as a judge for three years before enlisting for the Marines during World War II. After the war, he won the Republican nomination in 1946 and was elected that autumn and again in 1952. His term ended with his death on 2nd May, 1957.

73. RONALD REAGAN

Ronald Reagan was a radio, television and film actor, who went on to become the 40th President of the USA. He was born on 6th February, 1911, in Illinois, USA. He studied economics and sociology.

Reagan became involved in politics and ran for the Governor of California. He was elected President in 1981. He is most famous for being President during the end of the Cold War with the Soviet Union. He passed away on 5th June, 2004.

74. BARACK OBAMA

Barack Obama was the 44th President of the USA and the first African American to hold the office. He was born on 4th August, 1961. He graduated with a degree in Political Science from Columbia University, New York City, in 1983.

For a few years after graduating, he worked as a writer and editor for Business International Corp., a research, publishing and consulting firm in Manhattan. He went back to school three years later and graduated from the Harvard Law School in 1991.

After this, he moved to Chicago and became active in the Democratic Party. He initiated and organised Project Vote, a drive that encouraged thousands of African Americans to vote. In 1996, he was elected to the Illinois Senate. He kept moving up the ranks till finally, in 2008, he was elected as the President. He was re-elected as President in November, 2012.

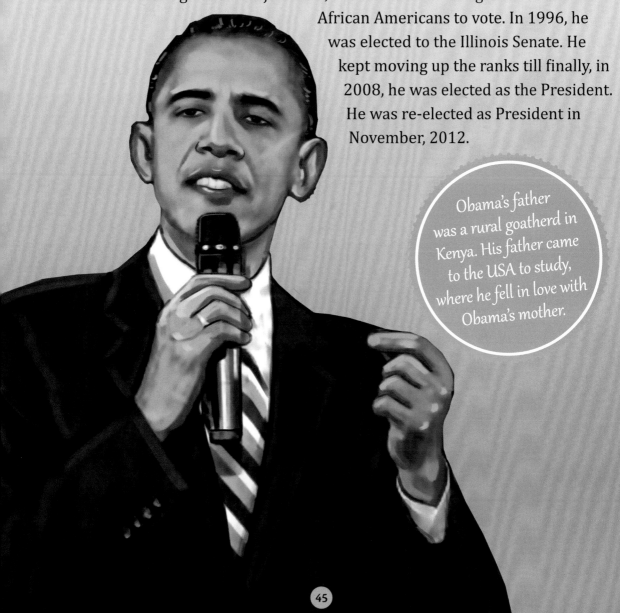

Obama's father was a rural goatherd in Kenya. His father came to the USA to study, where he fell in love with Obama's mother.

75. JIMMY CARTER

James Earl Carter Jr. is an American politician, who went on to become the 39th President of the USA. He was born on 1st October, 1924, in Plains, Georgia, USA. Carter attended Georgia South Western College and Georgia Institute of Technology. He completed his graduation from the US Naval Academy.

Carter started his political career when he stood for election for the Georgia State Senate. Later, he ran for President and was elected to the office in 1977. He is credited with adding two new departments in his cabinet—the Department of Energy and the Department of Education. Carter received the Nobel Peace Prize for his work in 2002.

76. BENAZIR BHUTTO

Benazir Bhutto was a Pakistani politician, who was the first woman leader of a Muslim nation in modern history. She was born on 21st June, 1953.

She served two terms as prime minister, one in 1988–1990 and other in 1993–1996. Her father, Zulfikar Ali Bhutto, was also a prominent Pakistani politician. She studied at Harvard University, graduating in 1973. She endured frequent house arrests between 1979 and 1984 and was even exiled for two years from 1984–1986. She returned to Pakistan after her exile. She was assassinated on 27th December, 2007.

77. KIM JONG-IL

Kim Jong-il was the Supreme Leader of North Korea for 17 years. He was born on 16th February, 1941, in Russia. He attended a pilot's training college for two years but graduated from Kim Il Sung University in 1963.

The official North Korean version of his life claims that he was born at the base of Mount Paektu, the highest peak on the Korean plateau. It also states that several auspicious signs, like a double rainbow in the sky, were sighted during his birth.

Kim Jong-il succeeded his father, Kim il-Sung, as the dictator of North Korea in 1994. Kim Jong-il is the third member of the family to lead North Korea. He was referred to as "Dear Leader". He was known to encourage the arts. Creativity in literature and films flourished during his tenure. He passed away on 17th December, 2011.

In order to create better films in North Korea, Kim had a South Korean director and his wife kidnapped and brought to the North, where they were forced to serve him till they escaped.

78. MARGARET THATCHER

Margaret Thatcher was the first woman Prime Minister of Britain. She was born on 13th October, 1925, in Lincolnshire, England. She studied chemistry from Oxford University and also practised as a barrister from 1954. Thatcher had great interest in politics.

Thatcher ran for the parliament in 1950, but was not successful. She was elected to the House of Commons in 1959 and worked her way up the ranks. Thatcher was elected as the Prime Minister in 1975. She was the only British Prime Minister of the 20th century to have held office for three consecutive terms. Thatcher introduced many social and political reforms to tackle unemployment. She stated that the individual should not be completely bound by the state and advocated privatisation of state owned enterprises, sale of public houses to tenants, limits on the amount of money printed, etc. Thatcher announced her resignation as Prime Minister in November 1990, but continued to influence national politics. She passed away on 8th April, 2013, in London.

All of Margaret Thatcher's theories, combined with her personal look and style, came to be known as Thatcherism. She was one of the most dominant political figures of 20th century Britain.

79. MARTIN LUTHER KING JR.

Martin Luther King Jr. was an American activist and humanitarian who was the leader of the African-American Civil Rights Movement. He was born on 15th January, 1929, in Georgia, USA. King earned a bachelor's degree in sociology and divinity. He finished his PhD from Boston University.

Martin Luther King Jr. experienced racism when he was young and decided to do something to put an end to it. He worked towards racial equality and equal rights for all in the USA. He was assassinated at the young age of 39 on 4th April, 1968.

80. MIKHAIL GORBACHEV

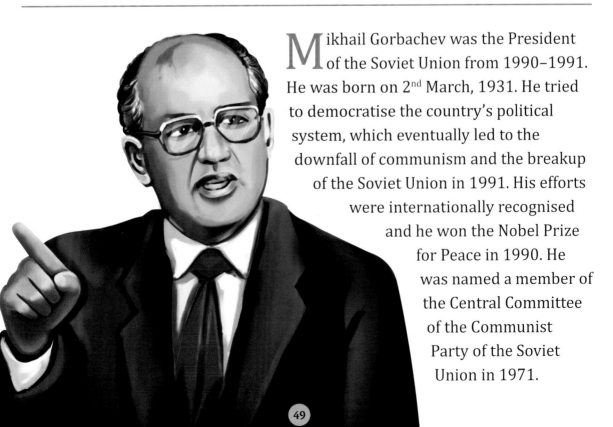

Mikhail Gorbachev was the President of the Soviet Union from 1990–1991. He was born on 2nd March, 1931. He tried to democratise the country's political system, which eventually led to the downfall of communism and the breakup of the Soviet Union in 1991. His efforts were internationally recognised and he won the Nobel Prize for Peace in 1990. He was named a member of the Central Committee of the Communist Party of the Soviet Union in 1971.

81. INDIRA GANDHI

Indira Gandhi was an Indian politician who served as India's Prime Minister for three consecutive terms and starteda fourth term that ended abruptly with her assassination. She was born on 19th November, 1917, in Allahabad, India. Indira Gandhi studied at Vishwa Bharati University in West Bengal and then at Oxford University in the UK. She joined the Congress Party in 1938. In 1942, she got married to Feroze Gandhi, a member of the Congress party. They had two children, Sanjay and Rajiv.

In 1947, the Congress Party came to power when her father took office, and she became a member of its working committee in 1955. Later, she was elected to the largely honorary post of party president. She was made a member of the Rajya Sabha in 1964 and that year, Lal Bahadur Shastri also named her as the Minister of Information and Broadcasting. She brought about a remarkable change in the country's economic, political, international and national policies. She was assassinated on 31st October, 1984, in New Delhi, India.

As a child, Indira decided to help the country. Alongwith her friends, she formed a monkey brigade who spied on police and distributed flags.

82. J F KENNEDY

John Fitzgerald Kennedy was the 35th President of the USA. He was born on 29th May, 1917, in Massachusetts, USA. He grew up in a powerful political family in Brookline, Massachusetts. In September 1941, Kennedy joined the US Navy. After the loss of his brother and brother-in-law, who were both defending their country, John ran for Congress in the early 1950s and won.

Kennedy ran for presidency in 1960 against then Vice President Richard Nixon. He won in one of the closest elections in history. He served as President from 1961 to 1963 until his assassination. He was assassinated in Texas on 22nd November, 1963.

83. FIDEL CASTRO

Fidel Castro was a Cuban revolutionary and politician, who also served as the Prime Minister and President of Cuba. He was born on 13th August, 1926, in Birán, Cuba. He began law school in 1945 and soon became interested in politics.

He organised a revolution to overthrow the government, but was unsuccessful and sent to prison. Once released, he planned his next revolution in Mexico. Castro overthrew Batista's government in 1959. In July 1959, Castro took over as leader of Cuba. He ruled Cuba from 1959 to 2008.

84. DONALD TRUMP

Donald John Trump Sr. is an American investor, author, television personality, real estate developer and business magnate. He was born on 14th June, 1946, in Queens, New York. He graduated from the Wharton School of Finance in 1968. He began his career at his father's company which focussed on middle-class rental housing. He soon became one of the most powerful landlords of America. He is the chairman and president of the Trump Organisation and the founder of Trump Entertainment Resorts. However, in the 1990s, he became bankrupt. He fought his way back to the top and wrote a book about it, called *The Art of The Comeback*.

Business Boomers

This section focusses on people who have become super successful by revolutionising businesses. Their work has contributed to providing opportunities to the world too. Let's find out not only about their success stories, but also their personal lives. Read on and get to know these business boomers.

85. HENRY FORD

Henry Ford was an American industrialist, who founded the Ford Motor Company. He was born on 30th July, 1863, in Michigan, USA.

At the age of 19, Ford made a tractor from an old mowing machine and a steam engine. Later, he developed a gasoline powered vehicle known as the Ford Quadricycle in 1896. It was a vehicle mounted on four bicycle wheels and looked like a horseless carriage. He then met Thomas Edison, who encouraged him to develop a better second model. "Model T" was launched in 1908 and was an instant success. Ford also developed a system of assembly line production that led to the mass production of cars. He passed away on 7th April, 1947.

86. MARK ZUCKERBERG

Mark Elliot Zuckerberg is an American computer programmer and entrepreneur who co-founded Facebook, a social networking website. He was born on 14th May, 1984, in New York, USA. Zuckerberg studied at the Phillips Exeter Academy. He used computers and started writing computer programmes in middle school. Later, he joined Harvard University in 2002.

While he was at Harvard, along with his roommates, he started a social website called facebook.com, where Harvard students could put in their personal details in a template he had developed. The website developed by Zuckerberg was different as it laid emphasis on real email addresses and names. He was helped by his roommates Dustin Moskovitz and Chris Hughes. Zuckerberg left Harvard to work on his new company Facebook. He launched Facebook in 2004 and by 2006, anyone with an email address could join Facebook. Facebook has more than 1.19 billion users now, making Zuckerberg a billionaire. The story of the birth of Facebook was depicted in the film *The Social Network*.

Mark Zuckerberg is colourblind and can't see the colours red and green. He can see blue though. Hence, the design of Facebook is in blue.

87. RICHARD AND MAURICE MCDONALD

Richard "Dick" McDonald and Maurice "Morris" McDonald were the founders of the world's largest fast food chain, McDonalds. Richard McDonald was born on 16th February, 1909 and his brother, Maurice McDonald, on 26th November, 1902, in New Hampshire, USA.

They started drive-in restaurants that specialised in serving burgers to its customers. In 1948, the McDonald brothers introduced the "Speedee Service System" which started the trend of the modern fast food restaurant as it is today. Maurice died on 11th December, 1971 and Richard on 14th July, 1998.

88. SAM WALTON

Samuel Moore Walton is an American businessman who founded the largest retail chain stores of America—the Wal-Mart Stores, Inc. He was born on 29th March, 1918, in Oklahoma, USA. He did many odd jobs while he was studying to make ends meet. He decided to open his own business after World War II, as he was always interested in retail.

He was given a loan of $20,000 by his father-in-law to open a variety store in 1945. He opened the first Walmart Store in 1962. He passed away on 5th April, 1992.

89. WARREN BUFFETT

Warren Buffett is an American investor and business tycoon who is believed to be one of the most successful investors of the 20th century. He was born on 30th August, 1930, in Nebraska, USA. Even as a child, Buffett enjoyed investing, earning and saving money. Buffett bought three shares of a company at the young age of 11.

Buffett graduated with a degree in Business Administration from the University of Nebraska, Lincoln. Buffett, at age 20, had earned almost $10,000 from his childhood businesses. He joined the Columbia Business School and earned a Masters degree in 1951. He formed his firm, Buffett Partnership, in his hometown, Omaha. Buffett invested in undervalued companies whose stocks shortly began to rise. This made him extremely rich and gained him the title— "Oracle of Omaha". In 1965, Buffett became a majority holder in the textile firm Berkshire Hathaway Inc., and it was the success of this firm that made him one of the wealthiest men in America.

In 2006, Buffett announced that he would give away 99% of his fortune to charity (about $62 billion), mainly to the Bill and Melinda Gates Foundation. Warren Buffett was awarded the Presidential Medal of Freedom in 2011.

90. RUPERT MURDOCH

Rupert Murdoch is an American-Australian entrepreneur and publisher as well as the founder of News Corporation, a media conglomerate. He was born on 11th March, 1931, in Melbourne, Australia.

Rupert Murdoch's father was a famous war correspondent and newspaper publisher. Murdoch first experienced the world of publication when he was the co-editor of his school journal. He inherited his father's papers, the News and the Sunday Mail. He quickly adopted a "sensationalist" style in all his newspapers. His papers were dominated by news of scandal and he often wrote the headlines himself. He bought many American newspapers in the 1970s. Murdoch also branched out into entertainment when he purchased 20th Century FOX Film Corp. in 1985 and launched the news channel, FOX News.

In 2011, Murdoch's companies, including "News of the World", regularly hacked the phones of several celebrities. He faced investigations for bribery and corruption by the British government and the FBI. On 21st July, 2012, Murdoch resigned as director of News National.

In 1993, Murdoch purchased Star TV, a pan-Asian television service based in Hong Kong, as part of his plan to build a global television network.

91. DHIRUBHAI AMBANI

Dhirajlal Hirachand Ambani was an Indian entrepreneur who founded Reliance Industries, which became one of the world's largest industrial empires. He was born on 28th December, 1932, in Gujarat, India.

Ambani started his career by working with a firm in the British Colony of Yemen in the 1950s. He moved to Mumbai in 1958 to start his own business of spices. After making minimal profits, he opened the first Reliance textile mill in Naroda, Ahmedabad and earned the title of "Prince of Polyester". Ambani established Reliance Industries in 1966, which now consists of more than 85,000 employees. He passed away on 6th July, 2002.

92. PHILIP KNIGHT

Philip Hampson Knight is an American business magnate and philanthropist who is the co-founder of Nike, Inc. He was born on 24th February, 1938. Knight graduated from the University of Oregon in Eugene, USA. He loved sports and was a runner himself.

Knight went to Stanford Graduate School of Business and realised that his true potential lay in being an entrepreneur. He co-founded Nike, Inc. In 1971, Knight and Nike helped start a sports business revolution in the 1970s that portrayed their new tennis shoes as symbols of athletic prowess and success.

93. LARRY ELLISON

Larry Ellison is an American businessman who is best known for co-founding the Oracle Corporation, an enterprise software company. He was born on 17th August, 1944, in New York, USA. He was given up for adoption by his biological mother when he was nine months old. He attended the Universities of Illinois and Chicago, briefly.

Ellison was inspired by a research paper written by computer scientist Edgar F. Cord that spoke of a relational database model. Ellison, along with Minor and Oates, worked and developed a program based on the same model. They released Oracle in 1979.

94. INDRA NOOYI

Indra Nooyi is the CEO of PepsiCo and the chairman of the board. She was born on 28th October, 1955, in Chennai, India. She graduated with a degree in chemistry from Madras Christian College in 1974 and got a Master's degree in Business Administration from the Indian Institute of Management in Kolkata, two years later. After coming to the USA, she pursued another Master's degree in Private and Public Management from Yale School of Management. In 2006, she became the first woman to lead this "Fortune 500" company.

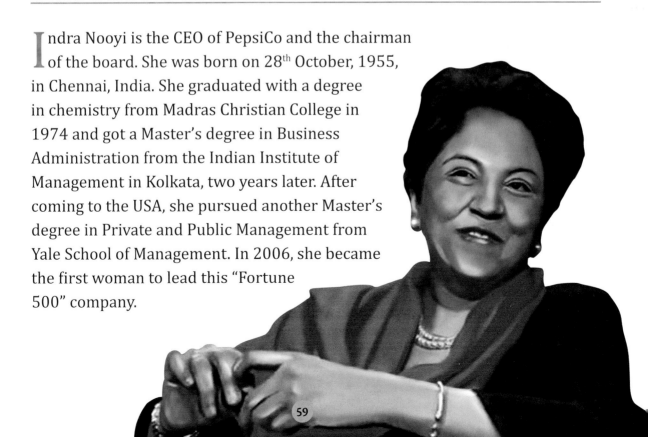

95. RICHARD BRANSON

Sir Richard Charles Nicholas Branson is an English investor, entrepreneur and the founder of the famous Virgin Group of companies that include 400 different companies. He was born on 18th July, 1950, in London, England. Branson was not very good at studies as he suffered from dyslexia.

Branson started a youth culture magazine called *Student* at the age of 16. He started a mail-order record company called "Virgin" to help fund his magazine efforts in 1969. He was then able to start a record shop on Oxford Street. By 1984, he became the majority shareholder in an airline which he later renamed Virgin Atlantic Airways. It started off with just a single aircraft but it survived in spite of stiff competition from established airlines.

In 2004, Branson formed Virgin Galactic, a space tourism company that is working towards offering commercial suborbital passenger flights.

Apart from owning a multi-million dollar business, Branson also holds records in powerboat racing and hot-air ballooning.

96. JEFF BEZOS

Jeff Bezos is an American entrepreneur and investor, who is famous as the e-commerce pioneer who started Amazon.com, Inc. He was born on 12th January, 1964, in New Mexico, USA. Bezos studied electrical engineering and computer science at Princeton University.

Bezos quit his lucrative job at an investment bank to open a virtual bookstore called "Amazon.com". Amazon.com became the leader of e-commerce and one of Internet's biggest success stories. Bezos purchased *The Washington Post* in a $250 million deal in 2013. This business boomer has broadened his market with Amazon offering the sale of videos, CDs, clothes, electronics, toys, jewellery and beauty products throughout the world.

97. STEVE WOZNIAK

Steve Wozniak is an American computer engineer and programmer. He co-founded the company Apple Inc. in partnership with his friend Steve Jobs. He was born on 11th August, 1950, in California, USA. He was fascinated by electronics at an early age. Steve Wozniak met Steve Jobs through a mutual friend during his brief stint at the University of California in Berkeley. Wozniak quit his job at Hewlett-Packard to team up with Steve Jobs and form Apple Computers in 1976.

> Steve Wozniak has been awarded an Honorary Doctor of Engineering Degree by various universities for his contributions to technology.

Wozniak only enjoyed engineering and not management. As many other engineers joined Apple, Wozniak no longer felt needed there. He ended his full-time employment with Apple permanently on 6th February, 1985, 12 years after having founded the company. Wozniak founded a new venture called CL 9, which developed and brought the first programmable universal remote control to market in 1987. In 2002, Wozniak founded Wheels of Zeus (WOZ), to create

wireless GPS technology. Wozniak published his autobiography, *iWoz: From Computer Geek to Cult Icon: How I Invented the Personal Computer, Co-Founded Apple, and Had Fun Doing It.*

98. STEVE JOBS

Steven Paul Jobs was an American inventor and entrepreneur who co-founded Apple Inc. He was born on 24th February, 1955, in California, USA. He was adopted at birth by Paul and Clara Jobs. The family moved from San Francisco to Mountain View, a suburban town in Santa Clara county, also known as Silicon Valley.

Jobs was introduced to Steve Wozniak by a mutual friend in 1970 with whom he shared a common love of electronics. Together, they created the Apple I and Apple II computers. While Jobs concentrated on the design, Wozniak took responsibility of the electronics. The Apple II was the first personal computer capable of colour graphics. Jobs insisted that Apple should design all the software and hardware of all Apple products.

Jobs started "Pixar Animation Studios" after he bought the computer graphics division of "Lucas film" in 1986. Jobs has been described as a perfectionist, brilliant, self-centred and temperamental. Not only was he a businessman and a technologist, he was also an artist and a designer. He passed away on 5th October, 2011.

Jobs was credited as the executive producer of the animated movie *Toy Story*.

99. NARAYANA MURTHY

Nagavara Ramarao Narayana Murthy is an Indian engineer, entrepreneur and an IT industrialist, who co-founded Infosys. He was born on 20th August, 1946. Murthy studied electrical engineering and M.Tech from the National Institute of Engineering, Mysore, and Indian Institute of Technology, Kanpur, respectively.

Infosys is an international firm providing engineering, consulting, technology and outsourcing services. Murthy was instrumental in the progress of the IT sector in India. He created many employment opportunities as well. Infosys was the first Indian company to be listed on the American Stock Exchange, NASDAQ.

100. MICHAEL DELL

Michael Dell is an American investor, author and entrepreneur, who is the founder of Dell, Inc., one of the leading manufacturers of personal computers. He was born on 23rd February, 1965, in Texas, USA. He was interested in technology since childhood. At the age of 15, he purchased an Apple computer and took it apart, just to see how it worked. When he was in college, he started building computers and selling them directly to people while focussing on cheaper prices and customer support. He started a personal computer revolution in the 1980s with the launch of the Dell Computer Corporation (Dell Inc).

101. BILL GATES

William Henry "Bill" Gates III is an American programmer, inventor and entrepreneur, who co-founded Microsoft Corporation with Paul Allen. He was born on 28th October, 1955, in Seattle, Washington, USA. Bill Gates wrote his first computer software programme at the age of 13.

Gates left Harvard to devote his career to Microsoft, a company he started in 1975 with his old friend Paul Allen. He started by developing software for micro-computers. Microsoft licenced an operating system named MS-DOS for use on IBM PC, i.e., personal computer. Gradually, all companies wanted Microsoft software and Microsoft went on to become the world's largest personal-computer software company. Gates is not only a tech guru, he is also a popular writer! *The Road Ahead*, his book, was published in 1995. He also wrote *Business @ the Speed of Thought*, in 1999, a book that shows how computer technology can solve business problems in new ways.

Bill Gates is believed to be one of the richest people in the world. In addition to his work, he is also famous for his charitable organisation, the Bill and Melinda Gates Foundation. It funds health programmes, provides study grants and many other programmes on global development.

102. PIERRE OMIDYAR

Pierre Omidyar is an Iranian-American entrepreneur, who founded the online auction website—eBay. He was born on 21st June, 1967, in Paris, France. Omidyar earned a degree in computer science from Tufts University in 1988. He worked for Apple and Macintosh before he founded eBay.

eBay is a multibillion-dollar online auction company that changed the course of online shopping and e-commerce. Omidyar was amazed at the number of buyers and sellers that his sight attracted. He was forced to start a new website which only focussed on auctions. By the end of 1998, it was one of the world's most profitable websites.

103. LARRY PAGE AND SERGEY BRIN

Larry Page and Sergey Brin are computer scientists, who co-founded Google, the online search engine. Larry Page was born on 26th March, 1973, and Sergey Brin was born on 21st August, 1973, in Moscow. Brin's family migrated to the USA to escape Jewish persecution in 1979, where he met Page at Stanford University.

They developed a new search engine technology, which they named "Google", based on the mathematical term "googol" which means 1 followed by 100 zeros. After its launch in 1998, Google has become the most popular search engine in the world.

104. JRD TATA

JRD Tata was an Indian businessman, who pioneered India's first airline and laid the foundation of Tata Group, India's largest industrial empire. He was born on 29th July, 1904, in Paris, France. JRD went to different schools in Paris, Mumbai and Yokohama.

JRD founded Tata Motors in 1945. He was the first licenced pilot in India and launched India's first international airline. He was the director of the Tata Group of companies that excelled in the field of technology, hospitality, chemicals, power, engineering and automobiles. He died on 29th November, 1993.

105. JOYCE C HALL

Joyce C Hall was an American businessman and co-founder of Hallmark Cards, Inc., which is the largest greeting-card manufacturer in the world. He was born on 29th August, 1891, in Nebraska, USA.

Joyce dropped out of high school with $3,500 that he collected by doing odd jobs. He went to Kansas City to seek his fortune. Hall arrived with two shoeboxes full of scenic picture cards in Kansas City. He hoped to sell it to dealers throughout the Midwest. With the money that Hall earned, he established a wholesale greeting-card business in Kansas City in 1910. He died on 29th October, 1982.

Greater Good

This section focusses on people who have worked for the betterment of society even if it meant sacrificing their freedom. Let's find out about their contributions and charities as well as about their lives. Read on and get to know these Miracle Workers.

106. MOTHER TERESA

Mother Teresa or "Blessed Mother Teresa of Kolkata", as she is popularly known, was a world famous humanitarian. She was born on 26th August, 1910, in Skopje, Republic of Macedonia. Her birth name was Agnes Gonxha Bojaxhiu. It is believed that Agnes loved the stories of the missionaries of Bengal. At the age of 12, she decided to commit her life to religion.

Agnes joined the Sisters of Loretto in Ireland in 1928. She then taught in an Order's school in Kolkata for 17 years. In 1946, she believed that she experienced a divine intervention that she was to devote her life to helping the poor and needy. Mother Teresa learnt basic medical training at Holy Family Hospital, Patna, and started helping poor people, especially in the slums of Kolkata. Mother Teresa founded the Missionaries of Charity, a religious congregation aimed to care for poor, ill and homeless people. She believed in extending care to all those people like lepers and cripples who felt unloved as they were shunned by society. She died on 5th September, 1997.

107. HARRIET TUBMAN

Harriet Tubman was an African American bondwoman who escaped slavery and then led the abolitionist movement. She was born in 1820. She worked as a maid, nurse, field hand, cook and woodcutter. She married a free black man. She then heard a rumour that she was going to be sold. She left her family and fled to Philadelphia. She later came back and freed her sisters and children from slavery. Over the next 10 years, she helped about 300 slaves to escape to Canada. She was sometimes called the "Moses of her people". She died on 10th March, 1913.

108. HELEN KELLER

Helen Adams Keller was an American author, political activist and lecturer, who was famous for being the first deaf blind person to earn a Bachelor of Arts Degree. Keller was born on 27th June, 1880, in Alabama, USA. She became blind and deaf when she was 18 months old. Her teacher, Anne Sullivan, played a very important role in her life.

Keller participated in many campaigns to raise awareness, money and support for the blind. She was appointed Councillor of International Relations for the American Foundation of Overseas Blind. She died on 1st June, 1968.

109. QASIM AMIN

Qasim Amin was an Egyptian jurist, who was most famous as the founder of the Cairo University as well as one of the founders of the Egyptian national movement. He was born on 1st December, 1863, in Egypt. He studied law from Khedival School and went to France for further studies.

Amin was a reformer, philosopher and judge who was famous for advocating women's rights. He was considered to be the "first feminist" of the Arab world. He died on 22nd April, 1908.

110. CLARA BARTON

Clarissa Harlowe Barton was an American teacher, nurse, pioneer and humanitarian, who is most famous for founding the American Red Cross. Barton was born on 25th December, 1821, in Massachusetts, USA. Barton was educated at home.

At a time when few women worked, Barton built a career helping others. She worked with a relief organisation known as the International Red Cross when she visited Europe. She proposed an American branch when she returned home and became the first president of the American Red Cross in 1881. Barton died on 12th April, 1912.

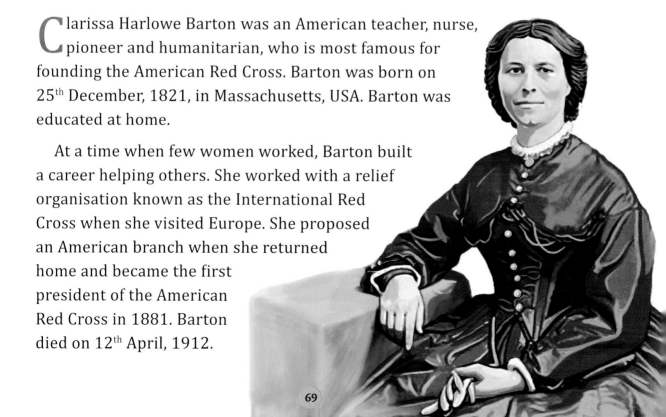

111. ELEANOR ROOSEVELT

Anna Eleanor Roosevelt was the longest-serving First Lady of USA, who was a writer and a famous humanitarian. She was born on 11th October, 1884, in New York City. She was sent to boarding school after the demise of her parents.

Roosevelt travelled thousands of kilometres to help those in need during the Great Depression. During World War II, she went to work for the Red Cross. She also represented USA at the United Nations (UN) for seven years and helped in drafting the Universal Declaration of Human Rights. She died on 7th November, 1962.

112. OSKAR SCHINDLER

Oskar Schindler was a German industrialist who is famous for saving 1,100 Jews from the Nazis. He was born on 28th April, 1908.

He started working with his father when he was just 16. He employed many Jews as his workers to save them from being killed by the Nazis. He gave away a lot of luxury items in bribes to save the Jews working in his factory. His factory was moved to Czechoslovakia. He made a list of 1,100 Jewish workers he thought were integral to his factory, submitted it to the Jewish Labour Office and took them with him. He then manufactured faulty arms that were engineered to fail. He died on 9th October, 1974.

113. RACHEL CARSON

Rachel Carson was an American marine biologist, humanitarian, environmentalist and writer, who played a significant role in spreading awareness about the environment movement. She was born on 27th May, 1907, in Pennsylvania, USA. She earned a Bachelors and Masters degree in Biology from Johns Hopkins University. She joined the US Fish and Wildlife Service in 1936. She conducted research on the effects of pesticides on the food chain and published it in *Silent Spring*, her most influential work. She died on 14th April, 1964.

114. JOHN PETERS HUMPHREY

John Peters Humphrey was a Canadian jurist, legal scholar and human rights advocate, who is most famous as the author of the first draft of the Universal Declaration on Human Rights. He was born on 30th April, 1905, in New Brunswick, Canada. He earned a degree in Bachelor of Arts, Bachelor of Commerce and Bachelor of Law.

Humphrey oversaw the implementation of 67 international conventions and the constitutions of dozens of countries during his tenure at the UN for 20 years. He passed away on 14th March, 1995.

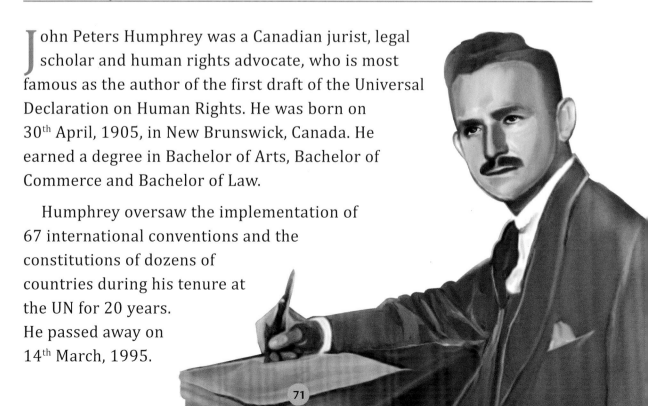

115. FLORENCE NIGHTINGALE

Florence Nightingale, often called the "Lady with the Lamp", was a social reformer, statistician and the founder of modern nursing. She was born on 12th May, 1820, in Florence, Italy. She assisted the ill and the poor from a very young age. She believed that nursing was her divine purpose.

Nightingale nursed the British and the allied soldiers during the Crimean War. She established the St. Thomas Hospital and the Nightingale Training School for Nurses in 1860 to formalise nursing. She turned hospitals into cleaner spaces and proved that trained nurses and clean hospit als helped sick people get better. She often walked around the wards at night, carrying a lantern in her hand, which is why she came to be known as the "Lady with the Lamp". She died on 13th August, 1910.

Florence Nightingale's math skills were as excellent as her nursing skills. She used statistics to better understand health care.

116. POPE JOHN PAUL II

Pope John Paul II was the head of the Catholic Church for 27 years. He was born as Karol Jozef Wojtyla on 18th May, 1920, in Wadowice, Poland. Wojtyla learned 12 languages when he was about 18 years old. He was ordained in 1946 and became the bishop of Ombi in 1958. In 1964, Wojtyla became the archbishop of Krakow. He was made a cardinal by Pope Paul VI in 1967. Wojtyla was elected Pope in 1978 and was the first non-Italian to become Pope in more than 400 years. He travelled to 129 countries during his pontificate and advocated human rights for all. He died on 2nd April, 2005.

117. MALCOLM X

Malcolm X was an African-American Muslim leader and a human rights activist, who worked towards the feeling of unity and belongingness amongst African-Americans in the USA. He was born on 19th May, 1925, in Nebraska, USA. He was involved in criminal activities during his teenage years. He underwent a complete transformation when he was in prison. He served as a spokesman for the Nation of Islam during the 1950s and 1960s. He passed away on 21st February, 1965.

118. FRANTZ FANON

Frantz Omar Fanon was a French philosopher, psychiatrist, revolutionary and writer who opposed colonisation. He was born on 20th July, 1925, in Martinique, France. Fanon was stationed at France during World War II. He trained as a psychiatrist in Lyon and took up a post in colonial Algeria.

Fanon joined the Blida-Joinville Psychiatric Hospital as a psychiatrist. It was here that he radicalised his methods of treatment and began socio-therapy, which was connected with his patients' cultural backgrounds. Fanon wanted to expose the serious repercussions of racial discrimination and proved the same through his psycho-therapy. He passed away on 6th December, 1961.

119. CHE GUEVARA

Ernesto "Che" Guevara was an Argentine physician, author, leader, diplomat, military theorist and Marxist revolutionary, who was a major figure of the Cuban revolution. He was born on 14th June, 1928, in Santa Fe, Argentina.
He completed his medical studies at the University of Buenos Aires and joined politics. He met Cuban revolutionary Fidel Castro and his brother Raul in Mexico, and helped them overthrow the Batista government in Cuba. He was killed by the Bolivian army on 9th October, 1967.

120. DESMOND TUTU

Desmond Tutu is a well-known South African activist and bishop, who was most famous for opposing apartheid. He was born on 7th October, 1931, in Klerksdorp, South Africa. After learning to be a teacher, he began to study theology and was ordained a priest in 1960.

In 1978, Tutu was appointed General Secretary of the South African Council of Churches. His efforts to solve the issue of inequality during the 1980s won him the Nobel Prize for Peace (1984). Throughout his life, he has been fighting for a democratic and just society without racial divisions.

121. KOFI ANNAN

Kofi Annan is a Ghanaian diplomat, who served as the seventh Secretary General of United Nations (UN) for nine years. He was born on 8th April, 1938, in modern day Kumasi, Ghana. Annan attended many schools and colleges and studied international relations in the USA and Switzerland. He started working for the UN as a budget officer for the World Health Organisation (WHO). He became an international civil servant and worked for the UN. Later, he became a special envoy to Syria.

122. ELLEN SIRLEAF

Ellen Johnson Sirleaf, winner of the Nobel Prize for Peace for her work towards women's rights, is a Liberian politician and economist who is also the President of Liberia. She was born on 29th October, 1938, in Monorovia, Liberia. Sirleaf studied accounts and economics at the College of West Africa and married James Sirleaf at the age of 17.

Sirleaf moved to the USA and continued her studies at the University of Colorado. She returned to Liberia in 1972 and began her political life by serving as the Assistant Minister of Finance from 1972–1973 under President William Tolbert, who represents the growing Americo-Liberian elite.

123. MUHAMMAD YUNUS

Muhammad Yunus is a Bangladeshi banker and economist, who is the co-recipient of the Nobel Prize for Peace in 2006. He was born on 28th June, 1940, in Chittagong, Bangladesh. He completed his Masters degree from Dhaka University. He also earned a PhD in economics from Vanderbilt University, USA.

He developed the idea of "micro loans", a system of credit loans for the poor and needy. These loans were given to people whose income was not enough to qualify for loans from banks.

124. AUNG SAN SUU KYI

Aung San Suu Kyi is the chairperson of the National League for Democracy in Burma, who was also awarded the Nobel Peace Prize in 1991. She was born on 19th June, 1945, in Rangoon, Burma. Her father, the de facto Prime Minister of the state that would be Burma later, was assassinated by his rival when she was two.

Suu Kyi completed her higher education at the University of Oxford. She spent more than 15 years of detention for her opposition of the military government in Burma. She gave many speeches calling for freedom and democracy and political activities across the country, and was chosen as the Leader of the Opposition in 2012.

125. MARGARET CHAN FUNG FU-CHUN

Margaret Chan Fung Fu-chun is a social activist and Chinese civil servant, who is the Director-General of the WHO. She was born in 1947 in Hong Kong. Chan studied home economics from Northcote College of Education in Hong Kong. Later, she obtained her medical degree at the University of Western Ontario, Canada. Chan earned her Master's degree in Public Health from the National University of Singapore as well. Chan joined World Health Organisation as Director of the Department for Protection of the Human Environment in 2003.

126. MARY SCULLION

Sister Mary Scullion is an American Roman Catholic Religious Sister, who is a famous activist for the homeless and mentally ill. She earned a degree in psychology from St. Joseph's University. She started working for the Sisters of Mercy in 1976. She is a co-founder of the Woman of Hope organisation that offers homes and support services to women who are mentally ill. She also upheld the cause of many other charitable trusts and foundations. She was ranked as one of the "World's Most Influential People" by Time Magazine in 2009.

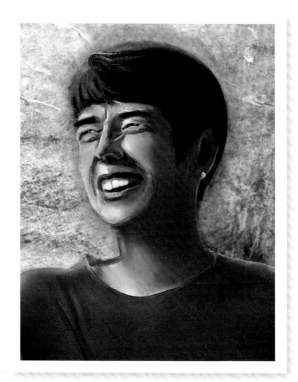

127. ASMA JAHANGIR

Asma Jahangir is a Pakistani lawyer who is an advocate of the Supreme Court of Pakistan and a human rights activist, famous for her work for the betterment of religious minorities, women and children. She was born on 27th January, 1952, in Lahore, Pakistan. She was born into a family with a history of human rights work and activism.

Jahangir has worked towards defending human and women's rights, rights of children and religious minorities in Pakistan. She is a founding member of the Human Rights Commission of Pakistan.

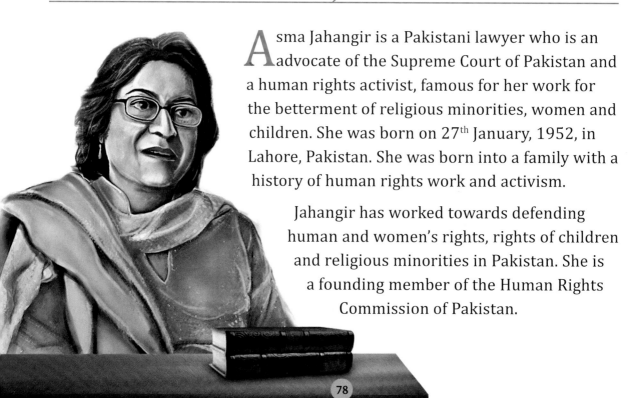

128. OPRAH WINFREY

Oprah Winfrey is an actress, philanthropist and one of the most popular television anchors who is famous for her talk show—The Oprah Winfrey Show. She was born on 29th January, 1954, in Kosciusko, USA. Winfrey graduated from Tenesse State University and secured a job as a co-anchor and reporter for ABC News in Baltimore.

Winfrey hosted a talk show named AM Chicago by a Chicago TV station, which became very popular. She then started her own talk show, "The Oprah Winfrey Show", which made her one of the most popular and richest people in the USA. The Oprah Winfrey Show was aired for almost two and a half decades.

Winfrey is listed as the world's richest woman of the 20th century by the Forbes magazine. She has also been hailed as the most influential woman of her generation. She founded Oprah's Angel Network that supports many charitable organisations.

Winfrey has co-authored five books and runs a magazine named O, the Oprah Magazine. She has also lent her name to animated films like Charlotte's Web and Princess and the Frog.

129. PRINCESS DIANA

Diana, Princess of Wales, was the first wife of Prince Charles, the heir apparent to Queen Elizabeth II. She was born as Diana Spencer on 1st July, 1961. Although she was not good at academics, she was an accomplished pianist. Diana married Prince Charles on 29th July, 1981. She was one of the most loved and adored members of the British royal family.

Princess Diana used her international celebrity status to help raise awareness about illnesses, poverty, drug abuse and homelessness. She upheld the cause of AIDS, child abuse and leprosy. Princess Diana founded as well as associated herself with many charities. Even after her divorce from Prince Charles in 1996, she continued to work for different charitable organisations. Princess Diana was deeply involved in efforts to ban land mines.

Her popularity as a member of the Royal family brought unprecedented attention to her public and private life. She became one of the most photographed personalities in the world.

Diana was killed in a car accident while trying to evade journalists on 31st August, 1997, in Paris, France.

Princess Diana's first autobiography was called *Diana: Her True Story* and was published in June 1992, while its sequel, *Diana: Her New Life*, was published in 1994.

130. CHEN GUANGCHENG

Chen Guangcheng is a visually challenged Chinese civil rights activist, who is best known for exposing abuses in the official family planning policies of China. He was born on 12th November, 1971. Guangcheng spent more than four years in prison on charges of disturbing public order. He was also under house arrest in his village of Dongshigu in Shandong province from September 2010 to April 2012, after which he fled to the US embassy in Beijing. After negotiations between the USA and China, he left for the USA, where he intended to study at New York University.

131. MELINDA GATES

Melinda Gates is an American businesswoman and philanthropist, who is also the wife of Bill Gates, the co-founder of Microsoft. She was born on 15th August, 1964, in Texas, USA. She earned her degree in computer science and economics from Duke University.

Gates is the co-founder of the Bill and Melinda Gates Foundation. She is working towards providing lifesaving medicine and basic, good quality education to children all around the world. Melinda Gates was ranked third in the Forbes list of the 100 Most Powerful Women in 2013.

Phenomenal Philosophers

There are some people who have influenced the world with their ideas and ways of thinking. Some of these philosophers were well ahead of their time. Read on to find out all about their ideas, ideals and personal lives.

132. SOCRATES

Socrates was a Greek philosopher whose thoughts and ideas have greatly influenced modern philosophy. He was born in Athens in 469 BCE. Although Socrates did not write any books himself, we know of his philosophies through the writings of his contemporaries and students like Plato, Aristotle and Aristophanes.

Socrates became famous because he went around Athens asking questions like "What is beauty?", "What is wisdom?" and "What is the right thing to do?". He was the first to question the purpose of life.

His questions made him a controversial figure and the comic dramatists of Athens often mocked him and his beliefs. He was sentenced to death for corrupting the youth of Athens in 399 BCE.

133. ARISTOTLE

Aristotle was an ancient Greek philosopher and scientist, who is considered to be one of the greatest intellectual figures of Western history. He was born in 384 BCE in Greece. He is considered to have laid the foundation for Christian and Islamic philosophy. Aristotle's theories and philosophies remained pertinent even after the Renaissance.

Aristotle studied under Plato at the "Academy" for 20 years. He wrote most of his theories in the form of dialogues. He wrote extensively during this period. Plato's influence on him is evident in his writings.

Aristotle believed that the dead are more blessed and happier than the living and to die is to return to one's own home.

Aristotle's intellectual range was vast. He covered many sciences as well as arts. He wrote about biology, botany, chemistry, ethics, history, logic, metaphysics, rhetoric, philosophy of mind, philosophy of science, physics, poetics, political theory, psychology and zoology. He died in 322 BCE.

Aristotle's father was the physician of Amyntas III, Alexander the Great's grandfather.

134. PLATO

Plato was a Greek mathematician and philosopher, who is believed to be the founder of modern science and philosophy. He was born around 428 BCE in Athens. Plato is believed to have been born in a wealthy family and educated in grammar and music. He was also a student of the great philosopher Socrates. Plato founded the "Academy," which is believed to be the first university or institute for higher learning in the world. Aristotle, one of the most famous philosophers of all time, was one of the students at the Academy.

Plato believed that everything happens for a reason. He believed that the perfect models of all things on the Earth existed in a world unseen by humans. He also believed that society would remain stable and fair only if philosophers were in power. He wrote down his teachings in different forms of conversations called "Dialogues".

Plato's work explored justice, beauty, society and equality. He questioned aesthetics, political philosophy, theology, cosmology, language and the philosophy of life itself. He died in 347 BCE.

Plato's real name was Aristocles. It is believed that "Plato" was a nickname given to him by his wrestling coach as he was big-built.

135. CONFUCIUS

Confucius was a famous Chinese teacher and philosopher, whose political theories and thoughts are popularly known as Confucianism. He was born around 551 BCE. He became interested in learning at the age of 15. He is believed to be the most learned man of his times. He became very famous and people sent their children to study with him. He is believed to be the first private tutor of China. He also worked as a shepherd, clerk and book keeper. Confucianism stresses the need to develop responsibility and morals through rigid rules of behaviour. He died in 479 BCE.

136. PYTHAGORAS

Pythagoras was a Greek mathematician and philosopher, who is most famous for his mathematical theorem called the Pythagoras theorem. He was born in Samos, Greece, around 570 BCE. He was interested in astronomy, philosophy, mathematics and music. He was very well educated and played the lyre as well.

Pythagoras studied triangles and perfect, odd and even numbers. He contributed to our understanding of triangles, angles, proportion, areas and polygons. The Pythagorean Theorem is believed to be the foundation stone of geometry. It simply states that the square of the hypotenuse (longest side of a right angled triangle) is equal to the sum of the squares of the other two sides. This theory has a number of practical uses in fields like trigonometry, oceanography, meteorology and geology. He died around 490 BCE.

137. NICCOLO MACHIAVELLI

Niccolo Machiavelli was an Italian politician, philosopher, humanist, historian and writer, who is believed to be the founder of modern political science. He was born on 3rd May, 1469, in Florence, Italy.

Machiavelli studied grammar and Latin. He went on many diplomatic missions and was responsible for the Florentine military as well. He became the secretary of the Florentine Republic. His most famous work, *The Prince,* brought him a reputation of being an atheist and an immoral person. He died on 21st June, 1527, receiving his last rites from the Church that he had bitterly criticised.

138. RENE DESCARTES

Rene Descartes was a highly influential French mathematician, philosopher, scientist and writer, who is considered to be the Father of Modern Philosophy. He was born on 31st March, 1596, in France. Descartes studied mathematics and physics. He studied law from the University of Poitiers.

Descartes believed that ethics was a science with its root in metaphysics. He focussed on moral and ethical behaviour. He also invented analytic geometry. He died on 11th February, 1650.

139. JOHN LOCKE

John Locke was an English philosopher and physician, who is known as the father of Classic Liberalism. He was born on 29th August, 1632, in Somerset, England. He studied medicine at Oxford University. He wrote about education, political philosophy and epistemology, which helped found modern Western philosophy.

Locke tried to determine the limits of human understanding based on the arguments of earlier philosophers. The writers of the American Declaration of Independence and Constitution have borrowed Locke's ideas. His writings influenced philosophers like Voltaire and Rousseau. He died on 28th October, 1704.

140. VOLTAIRE

Francois-Marie Arouet was a French writer, historian and philosopher, who advocated the separation of the state and the church. He was born on 21st November, 1694, in Paris, France. Francois-Marie Arouet wrote under the pseudonym "Voltaire". He wanted to be a writer even at a young age. His major work is divided into four categories: poetry, plays, historical works and philosophical works. He criticised intolerance, religion and the French institutions of his time. He was arrested and exiled many times. Voltaire is believed to have written more than 2,000 books and pamphlets. He died on 30th May, 1778.

141. DAVID HUME

David Hume was a Scottish philosopher, humanist and historian, who was famous for his philosophical empiricism and scepticism. He was born on 7th May, 1711, in Edinburgh, Scotland. He was 12 years old when he attended the University of Edinburgh. He thought of philosophy as the experimental science of human nature. Hume wrote about religion and was critical of some of the policies of the Church. He was famous for his six-volume book, *History of England. A Natural History of Religion* and *An Enquiry Concerning the Principles of Morals* are some of his works that were published after his death. He died on 25th August, 1776.

142. THOMAS PAINE

Thomas Paine was an English American author, political theorist and revolutionary, who was the author of two pamphlets that greatly influenced the American Revolution. He was born on 29th January, 1737, in Thetford, England. He studied reading, writing and arithmetic, and started working with his father at the age of 13. He wrote many articles, essays and pamphlets. His most famous 50-page pamphlet, *Common Sense*, sold 5,00,000 copies in few months. It influenced the American Declaration of Independence. He preached about war and its ill effects. He also spoke about religion and explained how it was not flawless. He died on 8th June, 1809.

143. IMMANUEL KANT

Immanuel Kant was a German philosopher, whose work on the "theory of knowledge" has influenced all subsequent philosophies. He was born on 22nd April, 1724, in modern day Kaliningrad, Russia. He studied theology and was attracted to physics and mathematics. He wanted to work on how the human mind worked and what reality is. During his time, some philosophers believed in empiricism, which means that knowledge comes from experience. Others believed in rationalism, which means that human reason makes sense of the world. He tried to bring the two groups together. He died on 12th February, 1804.

144. JEAN-JACQUES ROUSSEAU

Jean-Jacques Rousseau was a writer, political theorist and philosopher, whose work inspired the leaders of the French Revolution. He was born on 28th June, 1712, in Geneva. His first philosophical work, *A Discourse on the Arts and Sciences*, discussed the way in which arts and science had corrupted morality and virtue. He spoke about the stages of human development and other influences upon one's life. Rousseau preached about various fields from politics and science to inequality and social behaviour; he spoke about everything that affected the human being. He died on 2nd July, 1778.

145. J S MILL

John Stuart Mill was a political economist and a philosopher, whose theories inspired the people of the 19th century to a great extent. He was born on 20th May, 1806, in London. He studied extensively. He suffered a nervous breakdown at the age of 21 and turned to poetry for consolation, especially that of William Wordsworth. He started working on his philosophical views as well. He laid stress on the freedom of the individual from the state and equal rights for men and women. He died on 8th May, 1873.

146. GEORG WILHELM FRIEDRICH HEGEL

Georg Wilhelm Friedrich Hegel was a German philosopher who revolutionised European philosophy. He was born on 27th August, 1770, in Stuttgart, Germany. He studied philosophy and classics at Tubingen. After graduation, he became a tutor and an editor, and explored theology. Hegel is considered the last of the great philosophical-system builders of modern times. His philosophies were quickly politicised and set in opposition to champions of individualism such as Soren Kierkegaard and Karl Marx. He dealt with matters of social behaviour and its impact.

147. LEO TOLSTOY

Leo Tolstoy was a Russian author and philosopher, who is believed to be one of the greatest novelists ever. He was born on 9th September, 1828, in Tula Province, Russia. Tolstoy was educated at home and then went to the University of Kazan to study law.

He wrote his first book, *War and Peace,* in the 1860s. His second novel, *Anna Karenina* and *The Death of Ivan Ilyich* were some of his successful books. Tolstoy struggled throughout his life to understand the purpose and moral of life. His philosophies greatly influenced Mahatma Gandhi. He died on 20th November, 1910, in Astapovo, Russia.

148. KARL MARX

Karl Marx was a German philosopher, historian, economist, sociologist and a revolutionary socialist, whose theories and ideas are famous as Marxism. He was born in Prussia on 5th May, 1818. Marx studied the effect of social behaviour on one's psychological state. He joined as a staff of the newspaper *The Rheinische Zeitung* and soon became its editor in 1842.

When Marx was expelled from Paris, he went to Brussels and joined the Communist League. He published the famous pamphlet, *The Communist Manifesto,* in 1848. His book, *Das Kapital*, is also very famous. He died on 14th March, 1883.

149. SIGMUND FREUD

Sigmund Freud was an Austrian neurologist, who is known as the founder of psychoanalysis. He was born on 6th May, 1856. Freud was interested in literature and was well-versed in languages like Hebrew, Latin, Spanish, German, Italian and Greek. His understanding of the human personality was very different from earlier philosophers. Freud is regarded as one of the most controversial and influential minds of all times.

Freud's theory of psychoanalysis was based on resolving unconscious conflict through techniques like free association, dreams and fantasies. Freud's theories on the ego, the Oedipus and the Electra complex are some of his most influential theories. He influenced many other prominent psychologists like Erik Erikson, Alfred Alder, Carl Jung and also his own daughter, Anna Freud.

Although Freud's theories have been differently perceived by others, they have influenced and changed the field of psychology. He believed that all mental illnesses do not have physiological causes and was of the belief that cultural differences impact psychology and behaviour.

Sigmund Freud published his book, *The Interpretations of Dreams*, in 1899, which laid the foundation for the theories and ideas that helped him develop his psychoanalytic theory.

150. JIDDU KRISHNAMURTI

Jiddu Krishnamurti was a prominent Indian spiritual leader. He was born in 1895 in India. He was educated in theosophy by British social reformer Annie Besant.

He then became a teacher and writer. After the 1920s, he spent much of his time in the USA and Europe. In 1929, he separated from the Theosophical Society. However, he continued to be a popular lecturer. He believed in the importance of total spiritual freedom, which could only be attained through extreme self-awareness. He established Krishnamurti Foundations in the USA, Britain, India, Spain and Canada. He died in 1986.

151. AUROBINDO GHOSH

Aurobindo Ghosh was a famous Indian seer, poet and nationalist. He was born in the Indian city of Kolkata on 15th August, 1872. He started studying in a convent school in Darjeeling and completed his schooling in England. He continued studying languages in England at the University of Cambridge. He returned to India in 1892 and began studying Yoga and Indian languages, including Sanskrit. He was involved in India's struggle for freedom from the British rule and was even arrested in 1908. He fled to the French territory of Pondicherry in South India to escape the British. There, he founded an ashram (retreat) and developed a unique philosophy based on yoga. The ashram attracted students from all over the world. He died on 5th December, 1950.

152. MARSHALL MCLUHAN

Marshall McLuhan was an educator and communications theorist. He was born on 21st July, 1911, in Alberta, Canada. He studied at the University of Cambridge. McLuhan was a very popular professor and lecturer at the University of Toronto. His aphorism "the medium is the message" summarised the influence of television and computers in shaping human thought. He believed that once the electronic medium is used extensively, people would forget about books. He wrote about the invisible shackles of society. He died on 31st December, 1980.

153. NOAM CHOMSKY

Noam Chomsky is an American linguist, philosopher and activist, who is famous for his contributions in the field of language and mind. He was born on 7th December, 1928, in Philadelphia, USA.

He earned a PhD in linguistics at the University of Pennsylvania. Chomsky has been a professor for the Departments of Linguistics and Philosophy at MIT since 1955. His research has had huge ramifications for modern philosophers and psychologists, both raising and answering questions about human nature and how we process information.

Sports Stars

This section focusses on people who are remarkable sports persons. Their work has brought glory to the game and inspired many people who have watched them play. Let's find out about their skills and techniques as well as their lives. Read on and get to know these sport stars.

154. SACHIN TENDULKAR

Sachin Ramesh Tendulkar is a former Indian cricketer, who is considered to be one of the greatest batsmen of all times. He was born on 24th April, 1973, in Mumbai, India. Mischievous as a child, he was sent for cricket training as a punishment at the age of 11. Tendulkar started playing for the national cricket team when he was 16 years old. He is the only player to have scored a hundred centuries in international cricket. Tendulkar was a part of the team that lifted the ICC Cricket World Cup in 2011. He has been awarded Padma Vibhushan, India's second highest civilian award.

95

155. DON BRADMAN

Sir Donald George Bradman was an Australian cricketer, who is regarded as the greatest player of the 20th century. He was born on 27th August, 1908, in New South Wales, Australia. He scored his first century while playing for his school, when he was only 12 years old.

Bradman was the most popular cricketer during the 1930s and 1940s. He scored his first triple century against England at the age of 22. Bradman scored 6,996 runs for Australia at an average of 99.94 runs in every innings that he played. This average is unbeaten even today. He died on 25th February, 2001.

156. NADIA COMANECI

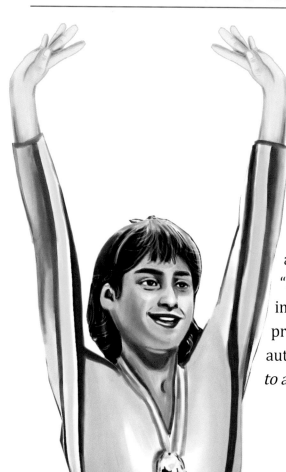

Nadia Comaneci is a Romanian gymnast, who is the first female gymnast to be awarded a perfect score of 10 in an Olympic gymnastic event. She was born 12th November, 1961, in Onesti, Romania. Comaneci took part in national junior championships in gymnastics when she was six years old. Comaneci won nine gold medals in the Olympics. The song that accompanied her floor exercises—called "Nadia's Theme"—won a Grammy Award in 1977. Now, Comaneci works towards promoting gymnastics. She has published an autobiography *Nadia* and a book named *Letters to a Young Gymnast.*

157. DIEGO MARADONA

Diego Armando Maradona is an Argentine footballer, who is considered to be one of the best football players of all time. He was born on 30th October, 1960, in Buenos Aires, Argentina. Maradona started playing football at a very early age. He started playing for the national team of Argentina 10 days before he turned 16. He was also a part of the Argentinean team that won the 1986 World Cup. He is best remembered for a goal scored with his hand during the World Cup, which the referee thought he hit with his head. It is now known as the "Hand of God" goal.

158. JOE DIMAGGIO

Joe DiMaggio was an American professional baseball player, who is considered to be one of the best all-round players of baseball. He was born on 25th November, 1914, in Martinez, California. DiMaggio started playing baseball at a very young age. He quit school when he was 14 years old and joined the minor league baseball team—San Francisco Seals. He joined the major league New York Yankees in 1936. DiMaggio holds the Major League Baseball record of a 56 game hitting streak. He retired in 1951 and was inducted in the Baseball Hall of Fame 1955. He passed away on 8th March, 1999.

159. JACK NICKLAUS

Jack William Nicklaus is an American professional golfer, who is considered to be one of the best golfers of all time. He was born on 21st January, 1940, in Ohio, USA. Nicklaus won the US Amateur Championship when he was studying at Ohio State University. He started as a professional in 1962 and won 18 major championships in a career span of over two decades. Nicklaus was one of the most dominant players on the PGA Tour. He designed several golf courses as well. Nicklaus wrote many books, including *Golf My Way* and *Nicklaus By Design*.

160. MUHAMMAD ALI

Muhammad Ali was a former American professional boxer, who was the first boxing champion to win the world heavyweight championship thrice. He was born on 17th January, 1942, in Louisville, Kentucky, USA. He took up boxing when he was 12 years old. Out of the 108 amateur games he played, he won 100. He became an Olympic gold medalist in 1960. His biography is called *GOAT—A Tribute to Muhammad Ali*. It weighs 34 kg and is covered in silk and Louis Vuitton leather. The first 1,000 books were sold at USD 7,500 each.

161. MARTINA NAVRATILOVA

Martina Navratilova is a former American tennis player and coach, who is one of three women to win a career Grand Slam in singles, women's doubles and mixed doubles. She was born on 18th October, 1956, in Prague, Czech Republic. Martina's stepfather, Mirek Navrátil, was her first coach.

She started playing professional tennis in 1975 and dominated the game for over a decade. When Navratilova won her 158th title, she had won more championship titles than any player in the history of tennis, male or female. She authored some books and was an active participant of the gay rights movement.

162. LARRY BIRD

Larry Bird is a former American basketball player, who is considered to be one of the best basketball players of all time. He was born on 7th December, 1956, in West Baden Springs, Indiana, USA. Bird attended the Indiana State University. He joined Boston Celtics and helped them win three NBA Championships, two NBA Final Most Valuable Player (MVP) Awards and the gold medal in the Barcelona Olympics in 1992. He is the only person in the history of NBA to be awarded MVP, Coach of the Year and Executive of the Year.

163. MICHAEL SCHUMACHER

Michael Schumacher is a former German race car driver, who is considered to be one of the best Formula 1 drivers of all times. He was born on 3rd January, 1969, in Hurth, West Germany. He was interested in go-karting as a child. He participated in the F1 race for the first time in 1991 for the Jordan team. He joined the Ferrari team in 1996. He won five consecutive F1 World Championships. He retired in 2006, only to come back and retire again in 2012. He is also an ambassador at UNESCO and is famous for his charity work.

164. KAPIL DEV

Kapil Dev Ramlal Nikhanj is a former Indian cricketer, who is the only cricketer to have scored 5,000 runs and taken 400 wickets in international test cricket. He was born on 6th January, 1959, in India. He played domestic cricket for his state, Haryana, and joined the national team when he was 28 years old. He is considered to be India's best fast bowler. He led the team to victory in the World Cup in 1983. He was a good all-rounder who batted well too. He was awarded the Padma Shri and the Padma Bhushan awards.

165. PELE

Pele is a former Brazilian footballer, who is considered to be the best football player of all time. He was born on 23rd October, 1940, in Tres Coracoes, Brazil. Pele started playing soccer as a teenager for a local club. He started playing for the national team when he was 16 years old. Pele was a part of three World Cup Championship winning teams. He holds the Guinness World Record for the most number of goals in the game of football. He has been named the World Player of the Century by the International Federation of Football history and Statistics. He is also known as "The Black Pearl".

166. SATCHEL PAIGE

Leroy Robert Paige, or "Satchel", was a legendary American baseball player, who is considered as one of the best pitchers in baseball history. He was born on 7th July, 1906, in Alabama, USA. Paige started playing baseball when he was 10 years old. He was well-known in the Negro Leagues and was finally allowed to play Major League Basketball in 1948.

Satchel's professional career lasted for 40 years. He is said to have played 2,500 games and won 2,000 of them. He was inducted in the Baseball Hall of Fame in 1971, the only player to have been selected on the basis of his play in the Negro Leagues. He died on 8th June, 1982.

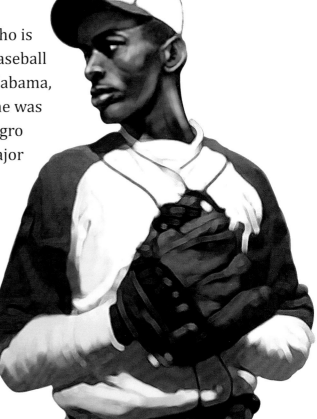

167. MICHAEL JORDAN

Michael Jeffrey Jordan is a former American professional basketball player, who is considered to be one of the greatest basketball players of all time. He was born on 17th February, 1963, in New York, USA. He played basketball, baseball and football as a child.

He studied at the University of North Carolina and was named the College Player of the Year. Jordan joined the Chicago Bulls in 1984. NBA has named Jordan the Most Valuable Player eight times. Jordan is nicknamed "Air Jordan" for his acrobatic moves and leaps while playing basketball.

168. SHANE WARNE

Shane Warne is an Australian cricketer, who is often regarded as the most effective bowler in the history of the game.

He usually bowls spinners and googlies (balls bowled with fingerspin that break unexpectedly in the opposite direction from that anticipated). His technique revived the forgotten art of leg spin and brought a variety to the game that had been dominated by fast bowling. In 2006, he became the first bowler to take 700 test wickets.

169. TONY HAWK

A nthony Frank "Tony" Hawk is a former American professional skateboarder, who is considered to be a pioneer in modern skateboarding. He was born on 12th May, 1968, San Diego, California, USA. He won more than 70 skateboarding contests in his career and is known as one of the top skateboarders in the world. He is nicknamed "the Birdman" and even started his own skateboarding company called Birdhouse. He has launched a series of successful video games and technical equipment. He is involved in philanthropic work through the Tony Hawk Foundation. He has authored several books, including his autobiography – *HAWK–Occupation: Skateboarder.*

170. STEVE DAVIS

S teve Davis is a professional snooker player, who changed the face of the game in the 1980s. He was born on 22nd August, 1957. He won the World

Championship a record number of six times and occupied the first rank for seven consecutive seasons. He won the English Under-19 Billiards Championship in 1976. He is known for the famous 1985 World Championship final against Dennis Taylor, which attracted a record breaking 18.5 million British viewers. He won his last world title in 1989 but has continued to play high-level snooker. Even at the age of 50, he is still ranked among the top 16 players.

171. STEFFI GRAF

Steffi Graf is a former German tennis player, who is famous as the only tennis player to win all Grand Slam singles championships and an Olympic gold medal in the same calendar year, which was called the Golden Slam.

She was born on 14th June, 1969, in West Germany. Graff was coached in tennis by her father from the age of three. She dominated world tennis for over a decade in the late 1980s and 1990s. Graff ranked World No.1 for a record 377 weeks, more than any other player, male or female. She married fellow tennis star Andre Agassi in 2001. She retired in 2009.

172. ANDRE AGASSI

Andre Agassi is a retired American tennis player, who was one of the dominant players of the 1990s and early 2000s. He was born on 28th April, 1970, in Las Vegas, Nevada. He started playing tennis as a toddler. He won many junior titles before joining professional tennis at the age of 16. He dominated the game for about 20 years. His competition with his arch rival, Pete Sampras, was very popular. He won career Grand Slam titles by winning all the major tennis tournaments. He retired from tennis in 1999.

173. PETE SAMPRAS

Pete Sampras is an all-round tennis player, who has won 14 grand slam titles. This was a record till it was broken by Roger Federer in 2009. Pete was born on 12th August, 1971.

During his career, he won seven Wimbledon singles championships, five US open titles and two Australian Open championships. He dominated professional tennis during the 1990s and is considered to be one of the greatest players of all time.

Pete started playing tennis after he moved to California in 1978. He joined the professional ranks in 1988 and by 1990, he was one of the top players. He retired in 2003 and was inducted into the International Tennis Hall of Fame in 2007.

174. MIKE TYSON

Mike Tyson is a former American professional boxer, who is famous as the youngest heavyweight champion in the history of boxing. He was born on 30th June, 1966, in New York. Tyson started professional boxing in 1985. His trainer, Cus D'Amato, taught him a new boxing style, eventually known as the "peek-a-boo" boxing style, holding his hands close to the cheek. He became the youngest boxer to win the WBC, WBA and IBF heavyweight titles when he was 20. He was inducted into the Boxing Hall of Fame in 2011.

175. SHAQUILLE O'NEAL

Shaquille O'Neal is a former American basketball player, who is famous as one of the heaviest players and for using his size and strength to overpower his opponents. He was born on 6th March, 1972, in New Jersey, USA. O'Neal studied at Louisiana State University and became one of the best players of the country while playing for them. He went on to become one of the most dominant players in NBA history, helping his teams to win NBA Championships. He was a part of the US basketball team that won the gold medal at the 1996 Olympics.

176. ZINEDINE ZIDANE

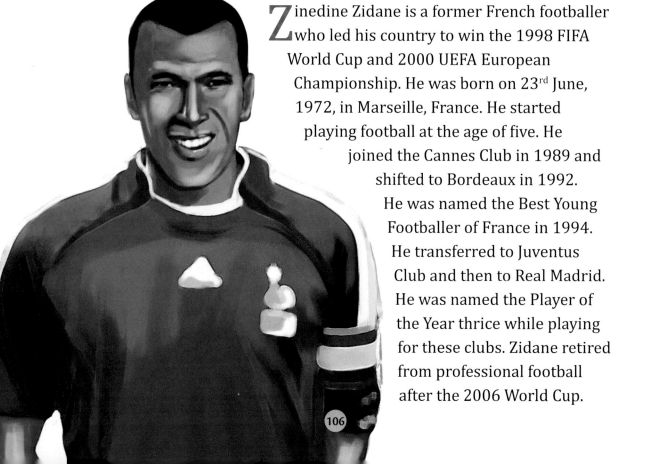

Zinedine Zidane is a former French footballer who led his country to win the 1998 FIFA World Cup and 2000 UEFA European Championship. He was born on 23rd June, 1972, in Marseille, France. He started playing football at the age of five. He joined the Cannes Club in 1989 and shifted to Bordeaux in 1992. He was named the Best Young Footballer of France in 1994. He transferred to Juventus Club and then to Real Madrid. He was named the Player of the Year thrice while playing for these clubs. Zidane retired from professional football after the 2006 World Cup.

177. JESSE OWENS

Jesse Owens was an American athlete, who is known as the most famous athlete of the 1936 Summer Olympics. He was born in Alabama, USA, on 12th September, 1913. His elementary school gym teacher noticed him run and was fascinated by his incredible speed. He first came to prominence when he won the world record as a tie in a 100 yard dash and jumped more than 24 feet in the long jump. Owens won four gold medals in the 1936 Olympics that were held in Berlin, Germany. He died on 31st March, 1980.

178. DAVID BECKHAM

David Beckham is a former English football player, who is considered to be one of the best football players in the world. He was born on 2nd May, 1975, in London, England. Beckham wanted to be a footballer since he was a child. In 1993, he started playing football for Manchester United, England's most famous soccer team. By 1996, Beckham was one of the most popular players as he helped Manchester United win the FA Cup and Premier Division title in the same year.

Beckham's pinpoint kicking accuracy has made him one of football's greatest stars. He became the fifth player in English history to play 100 matches. He retired from football in 2013.

179. TIGER WOODS

Tiger Woods is an American professional golfer, who is famous as the first golfer to win the four major tournaments of golf, namely the US Open, the Masters, the British Open and the Professional Golfers' Association of America (PGA) Championship. He was born on 30th December, 1975, in Cypress, California, USA. He started playing golf at the age of three. He turned professional in 1996 and has won 71 PGA tournaments till now. Woods has won about $110 million in prize money and is believed to be one of the richest sportspersons in the world today.

180. RONALDO

Ronaldo Luis Nazario de Lima is a former Brazilian footballer who is one of the three players in football history to be named the World Player of the Year thrice. He was born on 18th September, 1976, in Itaguai, Brazil. Ronaldo started playing football when he was 12 years old. He won the Golden Shoe Award in the 2002 World Cup as the highest goal scorer and helped Brazil lift the World Cup. Ronaldo's 15th goal in the 2006 World Cup made him the highest goal scorer in World Cup history. He retired from football in 2011.

181. THE WILLIAMS SISTERS

The Williams sisters are two American tennis players, Venus and Serena Williams, both of whom have been ranked as World No. 1 by the Women's Tennis Association. Venus Williams was born on 17th June, 1980, in California, USA, whereas Serena Williams was born on 26th September, 1981. They were both coached by their father and learnt to play tennis at a very young age. Serena and Venus Williams turned professional when they were 15 years old.

Serena and Venus Williams won gold medals at the Sydney Olympics in 2000 and the Beijing Olympics in 2008. In 1997, Venus Williams became the first unseeded tennis player to reach the finals of the US Open. Serena defeated Venus in the finals of the French Open, US Open and Wimbledon to win all three tournaments in 2002. Venus Williams has won seven Grand Slam titles and Serena Williams has won 17 Grand Slam titles.

Serena and Venus Williams have won all four Grand Slam doubles titles as a pair. They are the fifth pair in the history of tennis to achieve this feat.

182. ROGER FEDERER

Roger Federer is a Swiss tennis player, who is famous as the only player in the history of tennis to win 17 career men's single Grand Slam championships. He was born on 8th August, 1981, in Basel, Switzerland. Federer played badminton and basketball as a child to improve his hand-eye coordination. Federer began playing tennis when he was eight years old. He started playing professional tennis at age 17. Federer is the only player in history to have won the Wimbledon and the US Open consecutively for three years.

183. LEBRON JAMES

LeBron James is an American professional basketball player, who is the youngest player in NBA history to score 10,000 career points and win the Rookie of the Year award. He was born on December 30, 1984, in Ohio, USA. James played football in elementary school as well. He was a part of three US basketball teams for the Olympics that won one bronze and two gold medals. James has amassed a lot of name and fame with his endorsements and contracts. As of January 2013, he was the youngest player to score 20,000 career points.

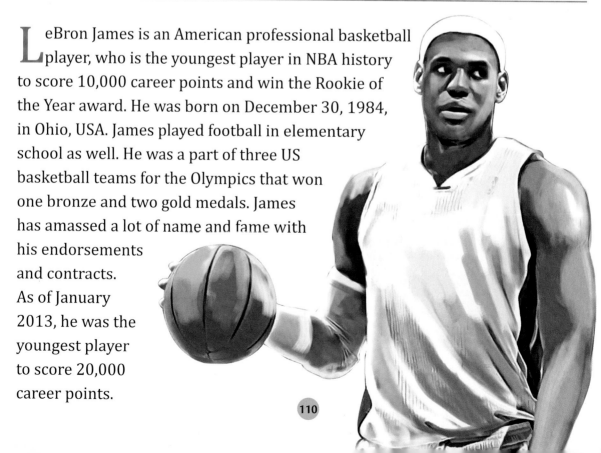

184. LIONEL MESSI

Luis Lionel Andres Messi is an Argentinean football player, who is rated as one of the best football players of all time. He was born on 24th June, 1987, in Rosario, Argentina. Messi plays as a forward for FC Barcelona and is the captain of Argentina's national football team.

Messi's talent drew attention from prestigious clubs and his family shifted to Barcelona when he was just 13. He started playing for FC Barcelona's under-14 team. Messi was the youngest official player to play in the Spanish La Liga at age 17. By the time he was 21, Messi was regarded as one of the best players. He has been named as FIFA Ballon d'Or or the world player of the year four times. Messi became the youngest player to score 200 goals for La Liga.

He scored his 233rd goal for Barcelona in 2012, becoming the club's all-time highest scorer at the tender age of 24! He was also named as the world player of the year for the fourth time in 2012, making him the only person to have won this title four times.

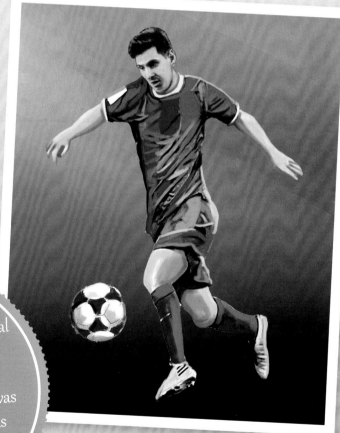

Despite his dual citizenship and professional success in Spain, Messi's ties with his homeland remained strong and he was a key member of various Argentine national teams from 2005.

185. USAIN BOLT

Usain Bolt is a Jamaican sprinter, who is the first athlete to win six Olympic gold medals in sprinting. He was born on 21ˢᵗ August, 1986, in Trelawny, Jamaica.

Bolt was interested in cricket and football when he was young. In fact, he was an outstanding fast bowler. But he was guided towards track and field by his coaches. Bolt won a gold medal for track and field racing when he was 15 years old. This made him the youngest person to ever win a world championship in any event.

By the time he was 17, he broke the junior world record for the 200 m run. He was also the first teenager to run it in less than 20 seconds.

In the 2008 Olympics, Bolt became the second athlete after Carl Lewis to win the 100 m, 200 m and the 4 x 100 m relay, and set world records in all three races. Bolt is believed to be the fastest man alive.

Bolt published a memoir, *My Story: 9:58: The World's Fastest Man*, in 2010. It was expanded and reissued as *The Fastest Man Alive: The True Story of Usain Bolt* in 2012.

186. MICHAEL PHELPS

Michael Fred Phelps II is a former American swimmer, who holds the record for the highest number of Olympic Gold Medals (18). He was born on 30th June, 1985, in Maryland, USA.

Phelps started swimming at the age of seven. At 15, he took part in the 2000 Summer Olympics. He went on to win medals at the Olympic Summer Games in Athens, Beijing and London, accumulating a total of 22 medals—18 gold, two silver and two bronze—setting the record for the most medals won by any Olympic athlete. Phelps announced his retirement in 2012.

187. RAFAEL NADAL

Rafael Nadal is a Spanish professional tennis player, who has been ranked among the world's top five players since 2003. He was born on 3rd June, 1986, in Manacor, Spain. He started playing tennis when he was four years old. He is the second male player after Andre Agassi to achieve the Career Golden Slam. When he won the French Open in 2013, he became the only player to win a single Grand Slam tournament eight times. He is believed to be the greatest player on a clay court that the world has ever seen.

Lights, Camera, Action!

This section focusses on people who have made significant contributions to the field of cinema. Let's find out about their talents and contributions, as well as about their lives. Let us see how the trends started by them have influenced people all over the world. Read on and get to know more about these celebrities.

188. ALFRED HITCHCOCK

Alfred Joseph Hitchcock was a film producer and director, who is famous for his suspense films. He was born on 13th August, 1899, in Leytonstone, London. Hitchcock entered the world of film as a draftsman for a film studio and quickly worked his way up to a director in 1925.

Hitchcock is famous for his movies, *Rebecca* and *Foreign Correspondent*, among others. He received knighthood in 1880 and is often said to be the greatest British filmmaker of all time. He died on 29th April, 1980.

189. CHARLIE CHAPLIN

Sir Charles Spencer Chaplin was a British producer, writer, director and comedian, who is considered to be the greatest comic artist in the history of world cinema. He was born on 16th April, 1889, in London, England. Chaplin's childhood was filled with hardships and he was sent to many workhouses as his mother was sent to a medical asylum.

Chaplin became a professional entertainer when he joined Eight Lancashire Lads, a clog dancing troupe. He also worked as a stage actor for some time. Chaplin joined the Fred Karno Company in 1908 and became famous for his work in *A Night in an English Music Hall*. While on tour in America, he got an opportunity to work for Keystone comedy films. Although the first film was not a great success, it was the second film—*Kid Auto Races at Venice*, where Charlie Chaplin improvised on his character and his immortal screen character "The Little Tramp" was born. Charlie Chaplin made great films like *The Kid, The Gold Rush*, and *The Great Dictator* among others. He died on 25th December, 1977.

Charlie Chaplin was the first actor to have had a comic strip made on him and also the first actor to have appeared on the cover of the Time magazine.

190. D. W. GRIFFITH

D.W. Griffith was a leading American director. He was born on 22nd January, 1875. His most famous films are *The Birth of a Nation* and *Intolerance*. He introduced many new techniques of storytelling and editing in his films, which soon became a norm in the film fraternity. His 1915 feature-length film, *The Birth of a Nation*, based on the civil war, was a blockbuster. But it was later criticised as being very racist. Film students study this film even today for its contribution to editing and storytelling techniques. His later work included *Intolerance, Broken Blossoms* and *Orphans of the Storm*. Griffith died on 23rd July, 1948.

191. WARNER BROTHERS

Albert Warner, Sam Warner, Jack Warner and Harry Warner are the founders of Warner Brothers Entertainment, Inc. Warner Brothers was started in 1923 and, since then, has become one of the biggest film studios in the world. They are a global leader in feature films; they release almost 20 films each year in over 120 countries. Warner brothers also has a television division, which has produced many successful shows.

192. LUMIERE BROTHERS

The Lumiere Brothers created the first motion picture camera and projector. They are the earliest filmmakers in history. Auguste Lumiere was born on 19th October, 1862, and Louis Lumiere on 5th October, 1864. They created the film *Workers leaving the Lumiere Factory*, which is considered to be the first movie. They also filmed the arrival of a train on a platform. It is said that people watching this film for the first time ran out of the theatre screaming as they thought that the train would burst out of the screen! The brothers opened cinemas in London, Brussles, Belgium and New York to show their films. Louis died on 6th June, 1948, and Auguste passed away on 10th April, 1954.

193. SHAHRUKH KHAN

Shahrukh Khan is one of the most sought-after Bollywood actors. He was born on 2nd November, 1965, in Delhi, India. He abandoned his studies to pursue acting. He began his career with theatre and television. In 1992, he starred in a movie, *Deewana*, which was the turning point of his career.

Khan began his career with anti-hero roles in movies like *Baazigar* and *Darr*, but moved on to play positive roles. He is famous for his work in Bollywood hits like *Dilwale Dulhania Le Jayenge*, *Kuch Kuch Hota Hai* and *Chak De India*, among others.

His acting won him many accolades, like the Padma Shri in 2005 and 15 Filmfare Awards.

194. VICTOR FLEMING

Victor Fleming was a film producer, cinematographer and director, who is famous for his work on the movies *Gone with the Wind* and *The Wizard of Oz*. He was born on 23rd February, 1889. Fleming entered the film business as a stuntman in 1910 and eventually got a job as a cameraman. He soon began directing and he was responsible for many of the films that would eventually be considered classics, such as *Treasure Island* (1934) and *Red Dust* (1932). He won an Academy Award for Best Director for the movie *Gone with the Wind*.

195. HUMPHREY BOGART

Humphrey DeForest Bogart was an American actor. He was born on 25th December, 1899. He is considered a cultural icon and the America Film Institute named him the greatest male movie star in the history of American cinema. He appeared in 75 films and became one of the finest motion picture "tough guys". His trademark on-screen personality was that of a hard-boiled cynic who eventually shows his noble side. He is famous for movies like *Casablanca, Dark Passage* and *The African Queen* for which he won his only Academy Award. He died on 14th January, 1957.

196. GEORGES MELIES

Marie-Georges-Jean Melies was a French magician. He is known as the father of special effects. He was born on 8th December, 1861. He accidentally discovered that he could use stop-motion photography to produce special effects and visual tricks. This could be called the beginning of special effects in film. Though he was not very well-known during his time, he paved the way for many other groundbreaking directors, like D. W. Griffith. He is sometimes called a "Cinemagician" because of his ability to manipulate reality through the lens of the camera. He made more than 500 short films in his lifetime. Two of his best-known films are *A Trip to the Moon* and *The Impossible Voyage*. Unrecognised, he died a pauper on 21st January, 1938, in Paris.

197. LUIS BUNUEL

Luis Bunuel was a Spanish filmmaker and director. He was born on 22nd February, 1900. Bunuel is famous for his surreal films and work in the Mexican Commercial Cinema. His early films, like *Un Chien Andalou* had a surreal, bizarre and dream-like quality to them. He developed very close relationships with painter Salvador Dalí and poet Federico García Lorca, and together, they formed the core of the avant-garde movement in Spain. He died on 29th July, 1983.

198. WALT DISNEY

Walter Elias Disney was an American filmmaker, producer, businessman and pioneer of animated cartoon films. Not only did he start Walt Disney Productions, he also planned and built Disneyland, the huge amusement park in Los Angeles, California. Disney was born on 5th December, 1901, in Chicago, Illinois, USA.

Disney was an innovator of animation. He shot to fame with his creation of the cheerful and mischievous Mickey Mouse. He went on to create more famous characters like Minnie Mouse, Donald Duck and many more.

The clever use of music and sound in his cartoons is what made Disney successful all over the world during the 1930s. The Disney Company is now one of the world's largest entertainment companies.

During his lifetime, Disney won 22 Academy Awards and received four honorary Academy Awards. He won seven Emmy Awards. He died on 15th December, 1966.

Walt Disney himself was the first voice of Mickey Mouse!

199. KATHARINE HEPBURN

Katharine Hepburn was an American film and stage actress. She was born on 12th May, 1907. She was known as a lively performer with a touch of eccentricity.

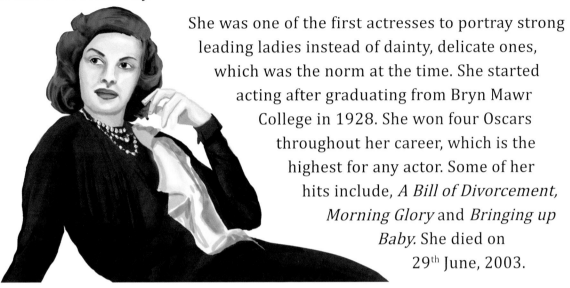

She was one of the first actresses to portray strong leading ladies instead of dainty, delicate ones, which was the norm at the time. She started acting after graduating from Bryn Mawr College in 1928. She won four Oscars throughout her career, which is the highest for any actor. Some of her hits include, *A Bill of Divorcement, Morning Glory* and *Bringing up Baby*. She died on 29th June, 2003.

200. WILFRED JACKSON

Wilfred Jackson was an animator, composer and director, who is best known for his work on *Mickey Mouse* and the *Silly Symphonies* series of cartoons. He was born on 24th January, 1906, in Chicago, Illinois. Jackson worked as an animator at Walt Disney Studios. He devised a method to synchronise animation with music during the age of silent movies. He is famous for his work on *Snow White and the Seven Dwarfs*, *Cinderella* and *Dumbo*. He died on 7th August, 1988.

201. AKIRA KUROSAWA

Akira Kurosawa was a Japanese film producer, director, editor and screenwriter. He was the first Japanese director to gain international fame. He was born on 23rd March, 1910, in Tokyo, Japan. Kurosawa went to art school after his higher education and aspired to be a painter. He worked as an assistant director in the PCL Studio in Japan and decided to pursue films as a career.

In 1943, Kurosawa directed, *Sanshiro Sugata*, which was very successful. However, *Roshomon* was probably his most famous film, even winning the Oscar for the best foreign-language film. Kurosawa directed 30 films in his 57-year film career. He died on 6th September, 1998.

202. WILLIAM HANNA

William Hanna was an animator, director, producer, cartoon artist and voice actor. He was born on 14th July, 1910. William Hanna and Joseph Barbera started Hanna-Barbera productions.

They are best known for creating Tom and *Jerry*. He also created other successful programmes such as *The Flintstones, The Jetsons, Scooby Doo* and *Yogi Bear*, to name a few. Hanna-Barbera won seven Academy Awards and eight Emmy Awards. Since then, their cartoons have been translated into more than 28 languages and have been aired all over the world. He died on 22nd March, 2001.

203. JOSEPH BARBERA

Joseph Roland Barbera is an animator, director, producer and cartoon artist. He was born on 24th March, 1911, in New York City. Joseph Barbera, along with William Hanna, founded Hanna-Barbera Productions. They became one of the most successful television animation studios, producing programmes such as *The Flintstones* and *Tom and Jerry*. Their cartoon characters are now considered cultural icons and have appeared in several films, books and toys. Together, Joseph Barbera and William Hanna have won seven Academy Awards and eight Emmy Awards. He died on 18th December, 2006.

204. ROBERT WISE

Robert Wise was a film director, producer and editor. He was born on 10th September, 1914. Wise has made films in almost every genre and is one of the most influential American movie directors. He is famous for films such as *A West Side Story, The Sound of Music* and *The Sand Pebbles*, among many others. Wise has won four Academy Awards, several lifetime achievement awards and also received the award for *Outstanding Contribution to Cinematic Imagery* by the Society of Motion Picture and Television Art Directors. He died on 14th September, 2005.

205. GREGORY PECK

Gregory Peck is an American actor, who is known for his portrayal of honest, straightforward characters. He attended a military school in San Diego State College before enrolling at the University of California at Berkeley to study medicine. It was here that he grew interested in acting and shifted to New York after graduation.

He studied at the Neighborhood Playhouse and supported himself by working as an usher at a music hall. He made his first Broadway debut in 1942 in *The Morning Star*, which was a flop though the critics liked his performance. Some of his famous films include *The Valley of Decision, Spellbound* and *Duel in the Sun*. He died on 12th June, 2003.

206. INGMAR BERGMAN

Ernst Ingmar Bergman is a Swedish writer and director. He was born on 14th July, 1918, in Sweden. He began his career as a screen writer, but later became famous for his film *The Seventh Seal*. He has won three Academy Awards for best foreign film. He soon became famous for his films that became the typical "art house" films of the 1960s and 1970s. His films include *Wild Strawberries* and *Winter Light*. He died on 30th July, 2007.

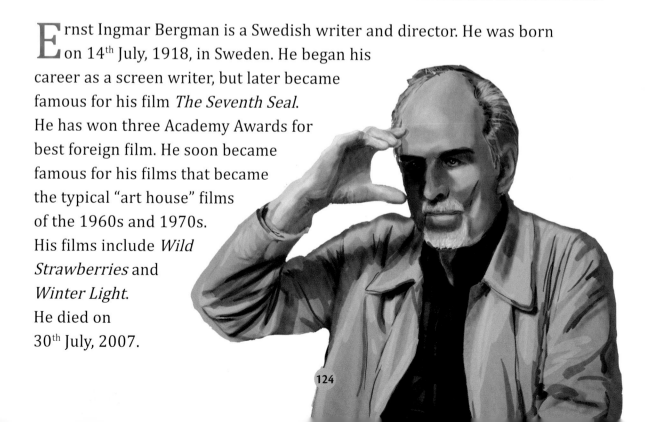

207. FEDERICO FELLINI

Federico Fellini was an Italian script writer and director, who was the first to blend fantasy images in his movies.

He was born on 20th January, 1920, in Rimini, Italy. He drew cartoons and worked for a humour magazine Marc Aurelio. Fellini joined director Roberto Rossellini and a team of writers to create *Rome, Open City*, a film that influenced the Italian Neorealist Movement. Fellini is famous for his movies, *Variety Lights, La Dolce Vita* and *8½*, among others. He won eight Academy Awards in his career. He died on 31st October, 1993.

208. SATYAJIT RAY

Satyajit Ray was an Indian script writer, movie maker, publisher, illustrator, graphic designer and film critic. He was born on 2nd May, 1921, in Kolkata, India. He began his career as a commercial artist and founded Kolkata's first film society in 1947. His first film, *Pather Panchali*, was an immediate success and won a Grand Prix at the Cannes Festival. His films were famous for their reflection of social reality. He received 32 Indian National Film awards in his lifetime. He died on 23rd April, 1992.

209. JEAN-LUC GODARD

Jean-Luc Godard is a film director, screen writer and film critic, who is famous for the French film movement in the 1960s called "New Wave". He was born on 3rd December, 1930. He studied at the University of Paris and worked at a job on a dam. It was the combination of these two things which inspired his first short film *Operation Concrete*, in 1958. Godard is often considered to be one of the most radical filmmakers of all time. In 2010, he was awarded an Honorary Academy Award. Godard continues to make controversial films to this day.

210. AUDREY HEPBURN

Audrey Hepburn was a British actress, who was known for her beauty and philanthropic nature. She was born on 4th May, 1929, in Brussels, Belgium. Hepburn studied in Holland and took ballet lessons as a child. Later, she went to Amsterdam and London to study ballet further. Hepburn started working in films when she was around 20 years old. It was her role as a ballet dancer in *The Secret People* that made her famous. Hepburn won the Academy Award for her role in the movie, *Roman Holiday*. She also worked as a goodwill ambassador for the United Nations Children's Fund or UNICEF. She died on 20th January, 1993.

211. FRANCOIS TRUFFAUT

Francois Truffaut was a French producer, director and film-critic, who was one of the founders of the New Wave movement. He was born on 6th February, 1932, in Paris, France. He was an avid reader but not a good student. He started working at the age of 14 and started a film club after a year. He won the prize for the best direction for his film *400 Blows* at the Cannes Film Festival. It also served as a major film for the New Wave movement. He died on 21st October, 1984.

212. ROMAN POLANSKI

Roman Raymond Polanski is a Polish film actor, writer, producer and director, who has made films in Poland, UK, USA and France. He was born on 18th August, 1933. Polanski was educated in Poland and started acting on stage at the age of 14. He acted in some films and studied film direction from the State School of Cinema in Lodz, Poland. Polanski made many films like *The Fat and the Lean, Repulsion* and *The Pianist* among others. Polanski has acted in and directed many theatrical productions.

213. WOODY ALLEN

Woody Allen is a film director, screenwriter, actor, comedian, musician, author and playwright, who is best known for his style of romantic comedy with a touch of parody and slapstick. He was born on 1st December, 1935, in New York, USA. Allen attended New York University in 1953, but failed the course in motion picture production. He dropped out and skipped several professions, including writing for television, stand-up comedy, music and play writing, before he finally started directing his films. He made his first film, *What's up, Tiger Lily?* in 1966. Some of his famous films are *Annie Hall, Manhattan, Hannah and Her Sisters* and *Midnight in Paris*.

214. GEORGE LUCAS

George Lucas is an American film director, producer and screenwriter, who created the famous space saga, *Star Wars*. He was born on 14th May, 1944, in California. Lucas was interested in racing as a career, but a near fatal accident changed his mind.

He was interested in film making since high school. He studied cinematography at the University of Southern California. He started his production house—Lucasfilm Ltd. Although his first films did not do well, his film, *American Graffiti* was a great success.

215. STEVEN SPIELBERG

Steven Allan Spielberg is a filmmaker, director and producer. He was born on 18th December, 1946, in Cincinnati, Ohio. He is considered to be one of the most influential and popular filmmakers in cinema. He has been in the film industry for over four decades. He became one of the youngest television directors for Universal in the late 1960s. A highly praised television film, *Duel*, brought him the opportunity to direct for cinema and he is now one of the most commercially successful directors of all time.

His movies range from science-fiction to historical dramas. He is famous for movies such as *E.T.: The Extra-Terrestrial* and *Schindler's List*. Three of Spielberg's films achieved box office records, becoming the highest grossing films made. He also won two Academy Awards for *Schindler's List and Saving Private Ryan*.

It's said that Spielberg had his first encounter with Hollywood when he sneaked out of Universal Studio tour and into the studio lot, where he met a helpful editor who showed him the basics of film-making.

216. JAMES CAMERON

James Cameron is a critically acclaimed film director responsible for some of the biggest box-office hits of this generation. He was born on 16th August, 1954, in Ontario, Canada. He eventually produced and directed some great films, including *The Terminator, Aliens, Titanic* and *Avatar*.

He studied art and later studied physics at the California State University in Fullerton. He tried his hand at several small jobs, including machinist and truck driver before he saw *Star Wars* and was inspired to make movies.

His large-scale, extravagant productions have earned him several Academy Awards. His most famous film is probably the 1997 hit, *Titanic*, which was the first film to earn more than $1 billion. It also got 14 Academy Award nominations, of which it won 11. Cameron won three Oscars for the project.

Cameron is a very good artist and actually drew a lot of the art pieces that featured so prominently in his film *Titanic*.

217. MATT GROENING

Matthew Abram "Matt" Groening is a cartoonist, animator, screenwriter, comedian, voice actor and producer. He was born on 15th February, 1954. Groening attended Evergreen State College and was the editor of the college newspaper. He is the creator of the comic strip *Life in Hell* and the television series *The Simpsons*. *The Simpsons* has been running for over 24 successful seasons and has won 10 Primetime Emmy awards. Groening has also won the British Comedy Award in 2004 and the National Cartoonist Society Ruben Award for his comic strip.

218. MICHAEL MOORE

Michael Moore is a filmmaker, author, social critic and political activist. He was born on 23rd April, 1954. He is best known for his documentaries, which are often controversial and address major political and social issues in the USA. He is famous for documentary, *Fahrenheit 9/11*, which is the highest grossing documentary of all time. His film, *Bowling for Columbine*, won the Academy Award for featured documentary. Moore has also written and starred in television shows such as *TV Nation* and *The Awful Truth*.

219. JOHN LASSETER

John Alan Lasseter is an animator, producer, director, screenwriter and the chief creative head at Pixar and Walt Disney Animation Studios. He was born on 12th January, 1957. He is a pioneer of modern animation, especially the computer-generated animation that was popular in the mid and late 1990s. Lasseter has directed films such as *Toy Story, A Bug's Life* and *Cars*. He won two Academy Awards for an animated short film titled *Tin Toy* and a Special Achievement in Animation Award for *Toy Story*.

220. TIM BURTON

Timothy Walter "Tim" Burton is a producer, director, writer, poet and stop-motion artist, who is famous for his horror and fantasy films. He was born on 25th August, 1958, in Burbank, California. He majored in Animation at the California Institute of Arts. Burton is well-known for his blockbuster films like *Edward Scissorhands, Beetlejuice, Alice in Wonderland* and *Charlie and the Chocolate Factory*, among many others. He has also written and published a poetry book titled *The Melancholy Death of Oyster Boy and Other Stories*. Tim Burton has won one Emmy Award and one Golden Globe Award.

221. JOE RANFT

Joe Ranft was a screenwriter, animator and voice actor, who is famous for his work with Pixar and Disney.

He was born on 13th March, 1960. He graduated from Monte Vista High School and went on to study character animation at the California Institute of the Arts. As one of the key creative members of Pixar Ranft, he helped create Disney classics like *The Lion King* and *Beauty and the Beast*. He is also known for his work on *A Bug's Life, Toy Story, Finding Nemo and Cars*.

222. JOHNNY DEPP

John Christopher "Johnny" Depp is an American actor, producer and musician, who is famous for his character Captain Jack Sparrow, in the movie series, *The Pirates of the Caribbean*. He was born on 9th June, 1963, in Owensboro, Kentucky, USA. He dropped out of school when he was 16 years old to pursue a career in music. He made his film debut in *A Nightmare on Elm Street* but it was the TV series, *21 Jump Street*, that made him famous.

He is famous for his roles in *Edward Scissorhands, The Rum Diary, The Ninth Gate* and *Alice in Wonderland* among others.

223. QUENTIN TARANTINO

Quentin Jerome Tarantino is a screenwriter, actor and director, whose films are famous for violence and sharp dialogue. He was born on 27th March, 1963, in Knoxville, Tennessee. Tarantino started training to act, but in 1990, he began his career as an independent film director. He is well-known for his movies *Pulp Fiction, Kill Bill, Reservoir Dogs* and *Django Unchained* among others. Tarantino's films have received many awards including two Academy Awards, two Golden Globe Awards and two British Academy of Film and Television Awards (BAFTA).

224. ANDREW STANTON

Andrew Stanton is a screenwriter, producer, voice actor and director, who is well-known for writing the movie *A Bug's Life*. He was born on 3rd December, 1965. After studying character animation at the California Institute of the Arts, he went on to join Pixar Animation Studios. Stanton co-wrote every film of the Toy Story series. He also worked on films such as *Finding Nemo, WALL-E* and *John Carter*, which was his first action movie. He has received two Academy Awards for Best Animated Feature.

Literary Lords

This section focusses on people whose names have been etched in the list of all time literary greats. Let's find out about their language skills and contribution as well as their lives. Read on and get to know these literary lords.

225. WILLIAM SHAKESPEARE

William Shakespeare was an English poet and playwright, widely regarded as the greatest writer in the English language and the world's best dramatist. Very little is known about Shakespeare's childhood, except that he was born in England on 23rd April, 1564. Over the course of 20 years, Shakespeare wrote plays that captured the complete range of human emotions and conflict.

Shakespeare wrote plays for the Lord Chamberlain's Men. He worked as an actor as well. His plays became very popular in London and soon, the Lord Chamberlain's Men were one of the most popular acting companies in the city.

These plays have been performed in countless hamlets, villages, cities and metropolises for more than 400 years. Some of his early plays include *The Taming of the Shrew, Richard III, Romeo and Juliet* and *A Midsummer Night's Dream.*

During his lifetime, Shakespeare wrote 37 plays and 154 sonnets! This means he produced around one and a half plays a year since he first started writing in 1589.

226. THOMAS WYATT

Thomas Wyatt was a 16th century English ambassador and lyrical poet. He was born in 1503 at Allington Castle, near Maidstone, Kent. He introduced the sonnet to English literature. Till then, it was common only in Italian literature. Most of his work consists of translations of literature from other languages. He also has a substantial number of sonnets to his name, though they were just imitations of sonnets written by the Italian poet, Petrarch. He died on 11th October, 1542.

227. JOHN LYLY

John Lyly was an author, who greatly influenced the style of prose writing in the English language. He was born around 1554. He is also known for moving away from the traditional poetic form of dialogues in comic plays to a more conversational style. He was known for his humorous plays and, after 1580, wrote only comic plays. In addition to the plays, Lyly also composed *Entertainment*, a show that combined elements of drama for Queen Elizabeth. He died in November, 1606.

228. DANTE ALIGHIERI

Dante Alighieri, commonly known as Dante, was an Italian poet, prose writer, political thinker and moral philosopher. He was born in June, 1265. He is best known for his epic poem, *The Divine Comedy*. This is a great work of medieval literature and examines philosophical questions of man's eternal destiny.

The poem is written in several sections which represent the three tiers of the Christian afterlife—purgatory, heaven and hell. The poem is often called the greatest literary work composed in Italian.

He made the conscious choice to write this poem in Italian and not Latin, as most scholarly works at that time were written. By doing this, he not only encouraged the common culture of his country, but also paved the way for Italian to become the literary language in Western Europe for many years to come. Dante died in September, 1321.

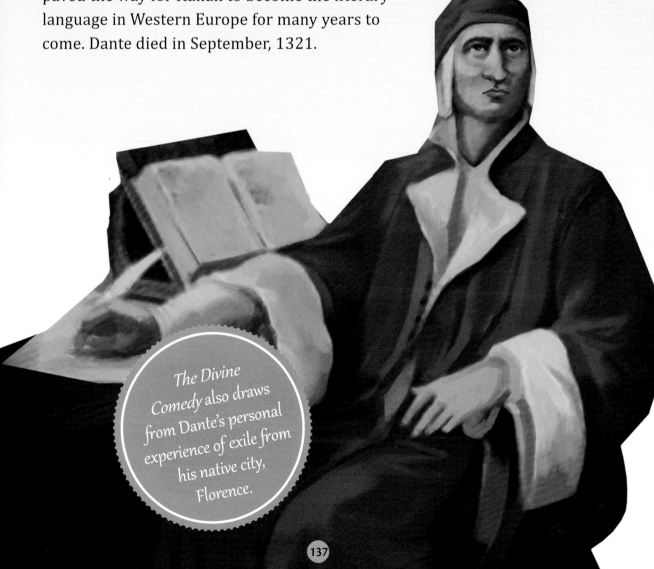

The Divine Comedy also draws from Dante's personal experience of exile from his native city, Florence.

229. FRANCIS BACON

Francis Bacon was an English philosopher and statesman, and a pioneer of modern thought. He was born on 22nd January, 1561, in London. He was the son of Sir Nicholas Bacon, keeper of the great seal for Elizabeth I. He studied at Cambridge University and Gray's Inn and became a member of parliament in 1584. However, he was not very popular during his time. He wrote several books and essays that argued for reformations of the law as well as religious, moral and civil meditations. He died on 9th April, 1626.

230. JOHN MILTON

John Milton is often regarded as one of Britain's finest writers, second only to Shakespeare. He was born in London in 1608. He received an excellent education, first with private tutoring, then a private school and finally Cambridge. Milton was a studious boy, who excelled in languages and classical studies. He is best known for his epic poem, *Paradise Lost*, widely regarded as the greatest poem in English. In his prose, he was strongly in favour of the abolition of the Church of England. His writings inspired not only the Civil War but also the French and American Revolution. He died on 8th November, 1674.

231. WILLIAM WORDSWORTH

William Wordsworth and Samuel Coleridge co-authored several "lyrical ballads" that helped launch a movement in literature known as the "Romantic Movement". He was born on 7ᵗʰ April, 1770.

He lost both his parents when he was just a child. He was sent off to a boarding school at Hawkshead, a picturesque village in the countryside. He grew up amidst the nature and greenery of the English lakes, which is reflected in his poetry.

He befriended a poet named Samuel Coleridge in 1797 and both of them co-published several poems. *The Rime of the Ancient Mariner* is one of their famous poems. Many of their poems broke the traditional form of long verses. Instead, they wrote short, dramatic lyrical poems. He was criticised for his low subjects and simplicity.

Some of his well-known poems are *The Tables Turned, I Wandered Lonely as a Cloud*, also known as *The Daffodils* and *Lines Written in Early Spring*. He died on 23ʳᵈ April, 1850.

Though Wordsworth's father was away from home for long periods of time, he encouraged Wordsworth to read. He even told him to memorise poetry written by Milton, Shakespeare and Spenser.

232. JANE AUSTEN

Jane Austen was a renowned English novelist, famous for her witty satires. She was born on 16th December, 1775. She started writing poems, stories and comics in order to amuse her family members. She collected all these into three bound notebooks, which are now called Austen's *Juvenalia*. The novel focusses on courtship and marriage. It is still known for its portrayal of the English society at the time. They depict her insights into the lives of women during the late 18th century and the early 19th century.

She first started writing around 1787. Between then and 1793, she wrote many plays, essays and short novels.

Her writing concentrates on the problems of women in those days and is what we would now call feminist in nature.

Some of her famous work includes *Pride and Prejudice, Sense and Sensibility* and *Emma*. She died on 18th July, 1817.

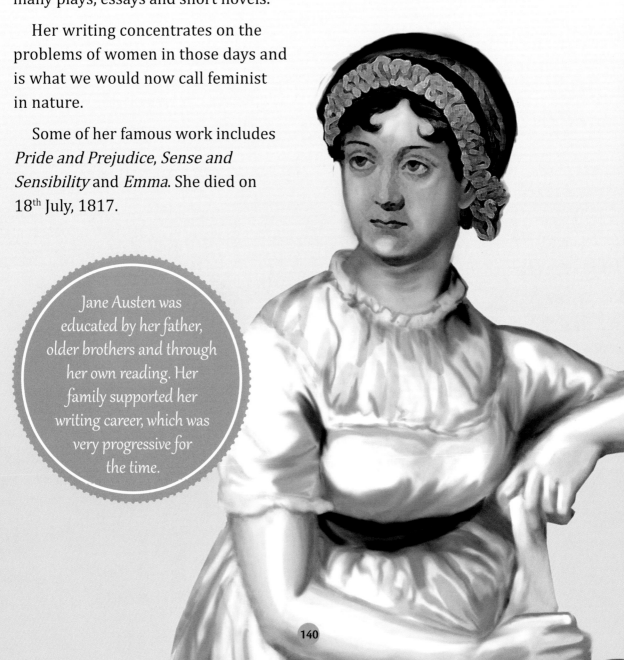

Jane Austen was educated by her father, older brothers and through her own reading. Her family supported her writing career, which was very progressive for the time.

233. JOHN KEATS

John Keats was a well-known English romantic poet. He was born in London, England, on 31st October, 1795. Though he did not receive much formal education, he was a voracious reader and developed a literary interest early in life. He had a difficult childhood and was forced to be an apprentice to a surgeon, but he left that job and devoted his life to poetry. He wasn't appreciated during his life, but his reputation grew after his death. Today, he is one of the most respected poets. He died on 23rd February, 1821.

234. EDGAR ALLAN POE

Edgar Allan Poe was an American author, poet, editor and literary critic, who is regarded as the inventor of the modern detective story. Poe was born on 19th January, 1809. Today, he is known for his mysterious tales of terror and haunting lyric poetry. He was the first American who tried to make a living solely through his writing. He was one of the earliest people to write mostly short stories. He was known for his own style of literary criticism. He is also considered to be a major contributor to early works in the science fiction genre. He died on 7th October, 1849.

235. CHARLES DICKENS

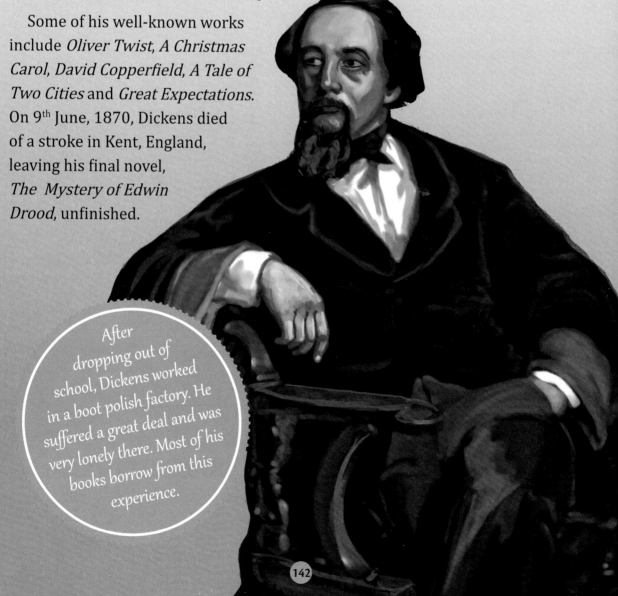

Charles Dickens was a British writer and social critic. He was born on 7th February, 1812. With 15 novels, five novellas and hundreds of short stories and articles, he is regarded as one of the most influential writers of the Victorian era.

He was forced to drop out of school and work in a factory when his father was thrown into prison. In 1836, he published *The Pickwick Papers* in weekly installments. It was a huge success and he shot to fame.

He published all his books in installments, since it allowed him to modify the plot and characters based on his audience's reaction. All his novels are known for their humourous and satirical style. They were often based on a keen observation of character and society.

Some of his well-known works include *Oliver Twist*, *A Christmas Carol*, *David Copperfield*, *A Tale of Two Cities* and *Great Expectations*. On 9th June, 1870, Dickens died of a stroke in Kent, England, leaving his final novel, *The Mystery of Edwin Drood*, unfinished.

After dropping out of school, Dickens worked in a boot polish factory. He suffered a great deal and was very lonely there. Most of his books borrow from this experience.

236. GEORGE ELIOT

Mary Anne Evans, who wrote under the pseudonym "George Eliot", was born on 22nd November, 1819, in Warwickshire, England. She enjoyed books and learning from a young age. She was introspective and quiet, so she was slightly different from the other young women of the time. George Eliot is considered by many to be one of the most important writers of the 19th century. She published all her translations, prose and poetry under her pseudonym, except for one. She died on 22nd December, 1880.

237. EMILY DICKINSON

Emily Dickinson was a famous poetess, who was unrecognised during her lifetime. She was born on 10th December, 1830. She enjoyed the poetry of Robert and Elizabeth Barrett Browning as well as John Keats. Dickinson was a very talented poetess and was known to write poems to her friends in letters. In fact, the first volume of her work was published in 1890, four years after her death. After she died, her family discovered 40 handbound volumes of nearly 1,800 poems. She died on 15th May, 1886.

238. LEWIS CARROLL

Lewis Carroll was an English logician, mathematician, photographer and novelist. He was born as Charles Dodgson on 27th January, 1832, in Cheshire, England.

He grew up in an isolated country village, but kept himself entertained. He had a difficult time in school and even got bullied because of his shy nature. He fell ill as a child and was deaf in one ear for the rest of his life. After schooling, he decided to continue studying. He got a scholarship at Christ Church, Oxford. He was exceptionally good at mathematics and graduated first in his class. He was offered a job and took up teaching at the college.

He would often entertain the dean's children by telling them stories that he would make up. One day, he told them about a little girl named Alice and her adventures underground. It was so good that they asked him to write it down for them. A writer, Henry Kingsley, happened to pick it up and read it. He convinced Carroll to publish it, which he did. It became so popular that he even wrote a sequel, *Through the Looking Glass*. He died on 14th January, 1898.

Lewis Carroll suffered from a stammer. But he found that he could speak fluently and naturally to children, which is why he enjoyed their company.

239. GEORGE BERNARD SHAW

George Bernard Shaw was an Irish playwright, who helped start the London School of Economics. He was born on 26th July, 1856. He tried his hand at all sorts of writing, including journalism, short story writing and novels. However, he was best known for his plays, which addressed social issues with a streak of comedy. He wrote more than 60 plays throughout his life and is known for his quick wit and sense of humour. His play, *The Apple Cart*, won him a Nobel Prize for Literature. But he is best known for his play, *Pygmalion*, which was adapted into the famous musical, *My Fair Lady*. He died on 2nd November, 1950.

240. ARTHUR CONAN DOYLE

Sir Arthur Conan Doyle was a Scottish writer and physician, who is known as the creator of Sherlock Holmes. He was born on 22nd May, 1859, in Edinburgh, Scotland. He studied to be a doctor. He settled in Portsmouth where he practised medicine and wrote stories. He first wrote about Sherlock Holmes in *A Study of Scarlet*, published in *Beeton's Christmas Annual* in 1887. It was a huge success and Doyle wrote more stories about the sleuth. Doyle had a varied career as a writer, journalist and public figure. He died on 7th July, 1930.

241. ROBERT LOUIS STEVENSON

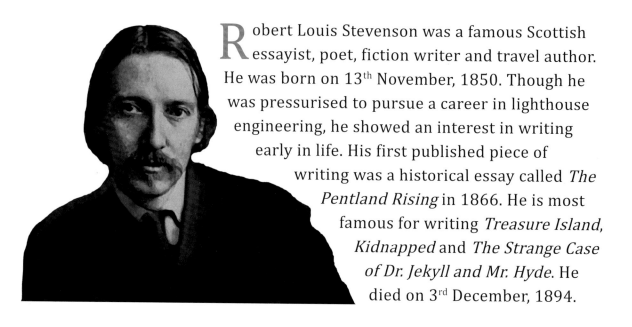

Robert Louis Stevenson was a famous Scottish essayist, poet, fiction writer and travel author. He was born on 13th November, 1850. Though he was pressurised to pursue a career in lighthouse engineering, he showed an interest in writing early in life. His first published piece of writing was a historical essay called *The Pentland Rising* in 1866. He is most famous for writing *Treasure Island*, *Kidnapped* and *The Strange Case of Dr. Jekyll and Mr. Hyde*. He died on 3rd December, 1894.

242. OSCAR WILDE

Oscar Wilde was a gifted poet and playwright, who was very popular in 19th century England. He was born on 16th October, 1854.

He was very progressive in his thinking and was known to preach the importance of style in life and art. He also attacked the narrow minded Victorian thought. Wilde is best known for his witty plays like *Salome, An Ideal Husband* and *The Importance of Being Earnest*. In spite of being a skilled writer, he only wrote one complete novel during his lifetime, *The Picture of Dorian Gray*, published in 1891. He died on 30th November, 1900.

243. MARK TWAIN

"Good friends, good books and a sleepy conscience: this is the ideal life."

Samuel Langhorne Clemens or Mark Twain was an American author, humourist, journalist, lecturer and novelist. He was born on 30th November, 1835. He gained international fame for his travel narratives, especially *The Innocents Abroad*, *Roughing It* and *Life on the Mississippi,* and for his adventure stories of boyhood, especially *The Adventures of Tom Sawyer* and *The Adventures of Huckleberry Finn*.

He began working as a typesetter and wrote articles for his brother's newspaper. He turned to journalism and published his first short story in 1865. It was an immediate success and he earned international fame.

Twain's early works were humourous light verses. But he started writing about more serious and harsh subjects later in his career. One of his most famous works in this category is *Huckleberry Finn*. The book combined humour and social criticism. He died on 21st April, 1910.

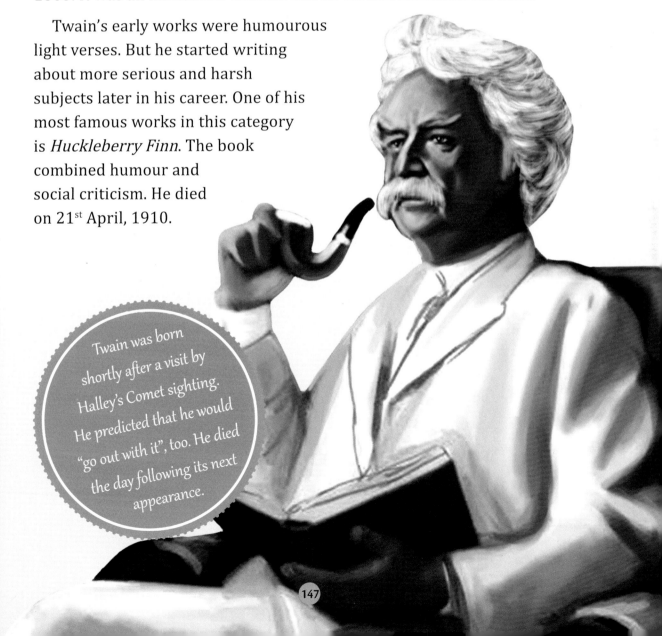

Twain was born shortly after a visit by Halley's Comet sighting. He predicted that he would "go out with it", too. He died the day following its next appearance.

244. RABINDRANATH TAGORE

Rabindranath Tagore was a Bengali poet, storywriter, essayist, playwright and artist from India. He was born on 7th May, 1861. He was awarded the Nobel Prize for Literature in 1913. He introduced a new form of story writing. He was also famous for using everyday terms in Bengali literature. He studied in England and is known for showcasing Indian art in the West and vice versa. Some of his most famous works are *Sonar Tari* and *Chitrangada*. He has also penned India's national anthem. He died on 7th August, 1941.

245. WILLIAM RANDOLPH HEARST

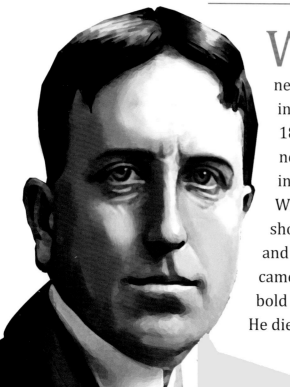

William Randolph Hearst was a newspaper publisher, who built the largest newspaper chain in America. He was born in San Francisco, California, on 29th April, 1863. He took over his father's struggling newspaper, *San Francisco Examiner*, and introduced a sensational style of reporting. Within the next two years, the newspaper was showing a profit. Competition with *Pulitzer* and the *New York World* gave rise to what later came to be known as "yellow journalism" with bold catchy headlines and exaggerated stories. He died on 14th August, 1951.

246. W. B. YEATS

William Butler Yeats was an Irish poet and playwright. He was born on 13th June, 1865, in Dublin, Ireland. He was one of the most well-known figures of 20th century literature. He made major contributions to both the Irish and the British literary establishments. He later served as an Irish senator for two terms. He was largely responsible for the Irish Literary Revival. He is one of the few writers who delivered their best work after winning a Nobel Prize. Some of these include *The Tower and The Winding Stair and Other Poems*. He died on 28th January, 1939.

247. VIRGINIA WOOLF

Virginia Woolf was an author known for experimenting with narrative structure. She was born as Adeline Virginia Stephen on 25th January, 1882, in London. She was brought up by very progressive parents. She began writing as a young girl and published her first novel, *The Voyage Out*, in 1915. She also wrote essays on artistic theory, literary history, women's writing and the politics of power. Her most popular novels are *The Voyage Out*, *Mrs Dalloway*, *To the Lighthouse*, *The Years* and *Between the Acts*. She died on 28th March, 1941.

248. EZRA POUND

Ezra Pound was an American poet and critic, who is known for his keen interest and advancement of the "modern" movement in American literature. He was born on 30th October, 1885, in Idaho, USA. In college, he studied language and literature. He went to Europe in 1908, where he published many books of poetry. During World War II, he broadcasted several pro-fascist programmes which led to his imprisonment. He died on 1st November, 1972.

249. T. S. ELIOT

Thomas Stearns Eliot was a poet, dramatist and literary critic. He was born on 26th September, 1888, in the USA. His literary work was appreciated by audiences worldwide. Some of his best known works include the poems *The Love Song of J. Alfred Prufrock, Murder in the Cathedral* and *The Hollow Men*. His most famous essay is *Tradition and the Individual Talent*. He has also made a name for himself in the field of literary criticism. In fact, some call him the greatest literary critic of the 20th century. He died on 4th January, 1965.

250. AGATHA CHRISTIE

Agatha Christie is one of the best-selling authors to date. She was born as Agatha Mary Clarissa Miller on 15th September, 1890. In 1914, she married Colonel Archibald Christie, a Royal Flying Corps pilot and took up nursing during World War I. She published her first book, *The Mysterious Affair at Styles*, in 1920. The story focussed on the murder of a rich heiress. Writing well into her later years, Christie wrote more than 70 detective novels as well as short fiction, selling over two billion copies. She died on 12th January, 1976.

251. J. R. R. TOLKIEN

J. R. R. Tolkien is credited with the revival of fantasy fiction for adults. He was born on 3rd January, 1892. He was a lecturer on English and literature, specialising in Old and Middle English. He did not write with the intention of getting published. He began writing his first published work, *The Hobbit*, as a story for his daughter. When it was published in 1937, it was an instant hit. His publisher asked for a sequel, which he delivered 17 years later. The sequel, called *The Lord of the Rings*, soon became one of the highest selling books of the 20th century. He died on 2nd September, 1973.

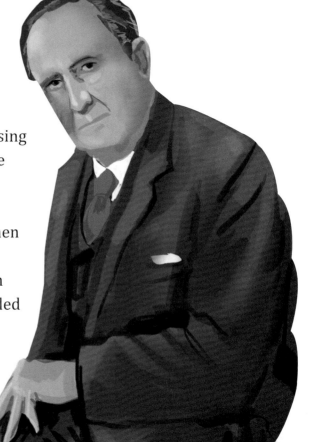

252. F. SCOTT FITZGERALD

Francis Scott Key Fitzgerald was a short story writer, who is considered to be among the greatest 20th century American writers. He was born on 24th September, 1896. His first novel, *The Side of Paradise*, was a great success that made him famous. Fitzgerald and his wife, Zelda, became important social figures. They moved to Paris, where he wrote his most famous novel, *The Great Gatsby*, in 1925. His later work was unsuccessful and he moved to Hollywood and became a scriptwriter. He died of a heart attack on 21st December, 1940, leaving his last book incomplete.

253. ERNEST HEMMINGWAY

Ernest Hemmingway was an American author and journalist. He was born on 21st July, 1899. He developed an interest in writing at a young age. He published many short stories before writing his first book, *The Sun Also Rises*. The book was well received by critics. His second major piece, *A Farewell to Arms,* became one of the most popular books in the World War I era. Hemmingway focussed on short stories following the war. During this time, he also wrote his only full-length play, *The Fifth Column*. He died on 2nd July, 1961.

254. ENID BLYTON

Enid Blyton is one of the world's most famous children's writers. She was born on 11th August, 1897. She is also one of the most prolific writers of all time, writing more than 700 books!

She is popular for her children's books, in which children have several adventures with little or no help from adults. Her books are still extremely popular across the world. They have been translated into about 90 languages.

As a teenager, her main interest had been writing poems, stories and other items. She had sent many of them to magazines, but none of them got published. She worked as a teacher, and began to have her articles about children and education printed in a magazine called *Teachers' World*. Her first book of poetry, *Child Whispers,* came out in 1922.

Her famous adventure series include *The Famous Five, The Secret Seven, The Five Find-Outers and Dog, St. Claires* and *Malory Towers.* For younger children, she wrote *Noddy, The Wishing Chair* and *The Magic Faraway Tree* amongst others. She died on 28th November, 1968.

Enid Blyton was 14 years old when she won a children's poetry competition. This encouraged her to submit articles, stories and poems to magazines.

255. GEORGE ORWELL

George Orwell was an English novelist, essayist, journalist and critic. He was born as Eric Arthur Blair on 25th June, 1903. He was the son of a British colonial civil servant. He studied at Eton, England, after which he joined the Indian Imperial Police in Burma, which was then under the British rule. He resigned in 1927 and became a writer. He moved to Paris in 1928 and eventually wrote the two most famous novels of the 20th century— *Animal Farm* and *Nineteen Eighty-four*. He died on 21st January, 1950.

256. TENNESSEE WILLIAMS

Tennessee Williams was an American playwright. He was born on 26th March, 1911, in Mississippi, USA. He was interested in writing plays while studying at the University of Missouri. He wrote plays through the Great Depression, while he was employed in a shoe factory. He first gained recognition in 1939, when his play, *American Blues*, won a Group Theatre award. He continued writing plays and finally, in 1947, his play, *A Streetcar Named Desire*, won a Pulitzer Prize. He also wrote two novels, essays, poetry, film scripts, short stories and an autobiography. He died on 25th February, 1983.

257. WALT WHITMAN

Walt Whitman was one of the most influential poets of the 20th century. He was born on 31st May, 1819. He was completely self-educated. His interest in reading was evident from a very young age. He read the works of Homer, Shakespeare and Dante as a child. He began teaching in a school at the age of 16 and founded a newspaper at the age of 19. His first novel and several short stories were published in 1842. However, he is best known for his collection of poems called *Leaves of Grass*, which are celebrations of the natural world. Whitman's most famous poem was inspired by Abraham Lincoln and named *Oh Captain! My Captain!* He died on 26th March, 1892.

258. ROALD DAHL

Roald Dahl is one of the most popular children's authors worldwide. He was born in Llanduff, South Wales, in 1916. After completing his schooling from Repton, a renowned British public school, he worked in Shell Oil in Africa. He enlisted in the Royal Air Force (RAF) when World War II broke out. He first wrote books that were targeted at adult audiences. He later published children's books, which made him famous. His famous works include *Matilda, Charlie and the Chocolate Factory, James and the Giant Peach* and *Fantastic Mr. Fox*. He died on 23rd November, 1990.

259. HERGÉ

Georgés Remi, whose pen name is Hergé, was born on 22nd May, 1907, in Etterbeek near Brussels, Belgium. He is credited with creating the comic strip hero Tintin, a teenage journalist. After 50 years, *Tintin's* adventures completed 23 albums and sold about 70 million copies in 30 different languages. He published his first comic strip— *Totor, de la Patrouille des Hannetons, "Totor of the June Bug Patrol",* when he was just 19. He created Tintin for the children's supplement, Le Petit Ventième of the daily newspaper Le Vingtième Siècle in 1929. It was in 1958 that The Black Island became the first Tintin album to be translated in English. He died on 3rd March, 1983, in Brussels.

260. SALMAN RUSHDIE

Salman Rushdie is a famous Anglo-Indian writer known for his allegorical novels. He was born on 19th June, 1947, in Mumbai, India. He is known for dealing with historical and philosophical issues through surreal characters and brooding humour in his novels. Rushdie stirred up a lot of controversy with his treatment of sensitive religious and political subjects. He is known for writing novels like *Midnight's Children, Shame* and *Satanic Verses.* The latter was declared as blasphemous and a fatwa was issued against Rushdie for the same, causing him to go into hiding for nearly a decade. His work on *Midnight Children* won him the Booker Prize in 1981. He was knighted in 2007.

261. TONI MORISSON

Toni Morisson was the first African-American woman to receive the Nobel Prize in Literature. She was born as Chloe Anthony Wofford on 18th February, 1931, in Ohio, USA. She graduated with a degree in English from Harvard University and went on to get a Masters degree from Cornell University. She came from a family that was extremely proud of their African-American roots and had immense respect for its culture, which is reflected in her books. Some of her well-known publications are *The Bluest Eye, Sula* and *Song of Solomon.*

262. DAN BROWN

Dan Brown is an American author, who gained popularity overnight with his novel, *The Da Vinci Code.* He was born on 22nd June, 1964, in New Hampshire, USA. He attended Phillips Exeter Academy and graduated from Amherst College. *Digital Fortress* was his first novel. He introduced the popular professor of symbology, Robert Langdon, in his next novel, *Angels and Demons.* Langdon reappeared in *The Da Vinci Code,* which was an extremely popular book that sold more than 80 million copies worldwide. The series was made into popular movies as well.

263. J. K. ROWLING

Joanne Kathleen Rowling is a famous author, who shot to fame for creating the famous Harry Potter series. She was born on 31st July, 1965. She went to Exeter University, after which she worked as a secretary and teacher, but then went through some tough times. Eventually, she was unemployed for a short period of time, during which she lived in poverty.

She wrote the first Harry Potter book, *Harry Potter and the Philosopher's Stone*, in 1997. The idea for the book came to her while on a train ride. She said that she really liked the idea of creating a place where a child could have power, like Hogwarts.

Even though about 50 publishers turned her down, she never gave up. Bloomsbury Publishing bought *Harry Potter and the Philosopher's Stone* in 1997 and it was an instant success. She eventually wrote seven books in the *Harry Potter* series, which were so successful that they were adapted into films.

J. K. Rowling published her first novel for adults, *The Casual Vacancy*, in 2012. She also wrote a crime novel called *The Cuckoo's Calling* in 2013, which she says is the first of a series.

Amazing Artists

This section focusses on people who have laid the stepping stone in the field of art. Their work has contributed to shaping the art world in a major way. Let's find out about their masterpieces and contributions as well as their lives. Read on and get to know these amazing artists.

264. LEONARDO DA VINCI

Leonardo da Vinci was an artist, scientist and inventor during the Italian Renaissance. He was born on 15th April, 1452, in Vinci, Italy. He is hailed as one of the most talented and intelligent people of all time.

Not much is known about his childhood, except for the fact that his father was a rich man. He worked as an apprentice with a famous artist named Verrocchio when he was 14 years old. He learned all about art, drawing, painting and more.

Da Vinci kept journals where he would draw and write about his scientific observations of the world. His journals were filled with diagrams of hand gliders, helicopters, war machines, musical instruments, various pumps and anything else that caught his fancy.

Da Vinci is regarded as one of the greatest artists in history. He has created several masterpieces throughout his lifetime, the most well-known of which are *The Last Supper* and *The Mona Lisa.* He died on 2nd May, 1519.

265. MASACCIO

Tommaso Cassai, known as Masaccio, was an Italian painter, who is sometimes called "the father of the Renaissance". He was born on 21st December, 1401.

In 1422, at the age of 21, Masaccio joined a group of painters known as the "Painter's Guild". He was given the nickname "Maso", meaning "clumsy". This was probably because of his absent-minded ways, his attire and his indifference towards worldly affairs. His paintings in the Brancacci Chapel of the Church of Santa Maria del Carmine in Florence remained influential throughout the Renaissance. He died in 1428 at the tender age of 27.

266. BOTTICELLI

Sandro Botticelli is one of the greatest painters of the Renaissance. He was born as Alessandro Filipepi in 1445 in Florence, Italy. He started out as an apprentice to a goldsmith. However, he soon got bored and decided to pursue painting instead. He then apprenticed with a painting master Fra Filippo Lippi. Botticelli learned a lot under Lippi. Botticelli is known for painting people, gods, goddesses and angels with dreamy looks on their faces. He is also known for his depiction of mythological scenes. He died in 1510.

267. DONATELLO

Donatello is one of the greatest sculptors of the Italian renaissance. He was born in Florence, Italy, around 1386. He was a master in both marble bronze sculptures. He was the son of a wool carver.

How he started his career isn't known. Some time between 1404 and 1407, he became a member at the workshop of Lorenzo Ghiberti. One of his earliest known works is a famous sculpture called *The David*. He became well-known early in his career.

By the time he was 20, he was getting paid for his work. While his work is very famous, not a lot is known about his personal life, apart from the fact that he was a man with very simple tastes. He is known for his lifelike, emotional sculptures. As a Renaissance sculptor, he is second to only Michelangelo. His knowledge of ancient sculpture was not matched by any other artist of his day. He died on 13th December, 1446.

Donatello's statue, *The David* was originally placed in the Cathedral and then moved to the City Hall, where it remained stood for a long time.

268. MICHELANGELO

Michelangelo di Lodovico Buonarroti, more commonly known by his first name, is perhaps the best-known Renaissance artist. He was born on 6th March, 1475, in Italy. He wanted to be an artist ever since he was a child. He was discouraged by his father from pursuing it because it was considered to be beneath the family status. His father had him enrolled in a school to prepare him for a career in business. However, Michelangelo was least interested in studying. Instead, he enjoyed copying paintings from churches and loved the company of other painters.

While studying, he met a student of painter Domenico Ghirlandaio, one of the most well-known painters in Florence, and took up an apprenticeship with him. But he left the apprenticeship after a year and studied under Lorenzo dei Medici, a retired sculptor.

Recognised as the most talented sculptor of central Italy, he was commissioned to carve the Biblical hero "David" for the Florence Cathedral.

He began his masterpiece, the 12,000 square foot ceiling of the Sistine Chapel, seven years later. Michelangelo died on 18th February, 1564.

Michelangelo didn't want to paint the ceiling of the Sistine chapel when the Pope first offered it to him. He was more interested in sculpting. However, today, it is considered to be one of his greatest works.

269. GIORGIO VASARI

Born on 30th July, 1511, in Tuscany, Italy, Giorgio Vasari was an architect and art historian. His book called *Lives of the Most Excellent Painters, Sculptors and Architects* is considered the foundation of art-historical writing. Vasari was the first art historian. He is called the "father of art history". He was also a renowned architect. He built and renovated many important churches and structures, including the Vasari Corridor in Florence. In 1547, Vasari built himself a beautiful house. After his death on 27th June, 1574, it has been converted into a museum dedicated to him.

270. GIAN LORENZO BERNINI

Gian Lorenzo Bernini was an Italian artist, who was the greatest sculptor and architect of the 17th century. He was born on 7th December, 1598. He is possibly the only artist to come close to Michelangelo's ingenuity. He is credited with creating the Baroque style of sculpture. Throughout his life, he served eight different popes. He contributed to several of Rome's landmarks, including St. Peter's Basilica and the Fountain of the Four Rivers. He died on 28th November, 1680.

271. RAPHAEL

Raffaello Sanzio da Urbino, better known as Raphael, was an Italian painter and architect from the Renaissance era. He was born in the year 1483 in Marche, Italy. Along with Leonardo da Vinci and Michelangelo, he forms what is considered the trinity of Renaissance masters.

Raphael was exposed to art right from his infancy, as his father was a celebrated artist. He studied under an artist called Pietro Perugino, whose influence was very evident in his early work.

He learnt from artists in Florence, while at the same time developing his own style. The biggest influence was of Leonardo da Vinci, who Raphael emulated in terms of complexity and poses.

Later, Raphael was commissioned by Pope Julius II to paint some of the rooms in Vatican. This was around the same time that Michelangelo was painting the ceiling of the Sistine Chapel.

He died on 6th April, 1520, at the young age of 37. As per his final wishes, he was buried at the Pantheon in Rome.

Raphael died on Good Friday. Some historians believe that he was also born on Good Friday, which fell on 6th April of the year 1483. But some are of the opinion that he was born on 28th March, 1483.

272. ANSEL ADAMS

Ansel Adams was a famous American photographer and environmentalist. He was born on 20th February, 1902. He is one of America's most loved photographers. He was known to work exhausting hours, sometimes more than 18 hours a day. He learned from and exhibited with other famous photographers of the time. Most of his important works were photographs of America's wilderness. His iconic black-and-white images helped to establish photography among the fine arts. He died in Monterey, California, on 22nd April, 1984.

273. SALVADOR DALI

Salvador Dali was a Spanish surrealist painter and printmaker. He was born on 11th May, 1904, in Figueres, Spain. He was adept at several styles. However, two events greatly influenced his style. He read Freud's work on dreams and the subconscious. He also met a group of Paris surrealists. The surreal movement in art and literature believed in the power of man's subconscious over reality. He often presented everyday objects in a dream-like absurd manner. Today, he is one of the best known surrealists of all time. He died on 23rd January, 1989.

274. ALBRECHT ALTDORFER

Albrecht Altdorfer was a Renaissance artist, painter and engraver. Born in 1480 in Germany, he worked in the town of Regensburg. He is credited with being the leading artist of the Danube School of painting. They used methods like etching to create works of art.

Altdorfer was the first painter to paint pure landscapes without any particular subjects. He also used anthropomorphism, which is the style of giving life-like characteristics to lifeless objects and plants.

However, his most famous works are Biblical scenes set against vivid, imaginative and colourful backgrounds. Intricate buildings portrayed in his paintings also showed off his architectural skill.

He created what came to be known by many as one of the most horrific paintings ever, *The Battle of Issus*. It shows the army of Alexander the Great storming into battle.

Altdorfer died on 12th February, 1538, in Regensburg, the place he was associated with all his life.

Albrecht Altdorfer's backdrops were beautiful, but not necessarily historically accurate. His painting, *A Cruxifiction*, which depicted the crucifixion of Jesus Christ, was set on the banks of a river!

275. REMBRANDT

Rembrandt van Rijn was a Dutch painter and printmaker. He was born on 15th July, 1606. He is well-known for telling stories through his paintings. He started out by painting portraits. Throughout his career, he continued to paint, etch and draw portraits. He was especially gifted at portraying people in their various moods and dramatic poses. He also enjoyed playing with light and shadow in his paintings. All his paintings reflected reality—he did not believe in beautifying his paintings, which earned him a lot of criticism. He died on 4th October, 1669.

276. JOHANNES VERMEER

Johannes Vermeer was a Dutch artist, who created some iconic images in art. Although only 36 of his paintings still survive, they occupy prestigious positions in the world's finest museums. He began his career in the 1650s by painting biblical and mythological scenes. But he is best-known for his later work, which depicts scenes of daily life in interior settings. Vermeer also painted cityscapes and allegorical scenes. Some of his best known works are *Girl With a Pearl Earring, The Milkmaid* and *The Astronomer*. He died on 16th December, 1675.

277. GUSTAVE EIFFEL

Gustave Eiffel is a civil engineer known for the construction of the Eiffel Tower. He was born on 15th December, 1832. He graduated from the College of Art and Manufacturing in 1855. After this, he began to specialise in constructing with metal and his early work focussed chiefly on bridges. The chief engineer on the Statue of Liberty died in 1879 and Eiffel was hired to replace him. He then began to work on the Garabit viaduct, the highest bridge in the world. After that, he started working on what would come to be known as the Eiffel Tower. The tower took two years to build, finally getting complete in 1889. The tower brought him the nickname "magician of iron". It also inspired him to take an interest in the problems of aerodynamics and he used the tower for many experiments. He also built the first aerodynamic laboratory at Auteuil, outside Paris. He worked here throughout World War I till he gave it to the State in 1921. Eiffel died on 27th December, 1923.

The Eiffel Tower is 320 m (1050 feet) in height and was the tallest artificial structure in the world for 41 years, before being surpassed by the Chrysler Building in New York.

278. ANDY WARHOL

Andy Warhol is an American artist and filmmaker. He was born on 6th August, 1928. He was an initiator of the Pop Art movement, which propagated the mass production of art and swept the USA in the 1960s. He studied fine art in college, after which he moved to New York City and began creating advertisements and illustrations for magazines. Warhol began creating the paintings he is best known for today in the 1960s. He loved pop culture and decided to paint what he loved. He painted large pictures of Coca-Cola bottles, Campbell's soup cans and dollar bills. He also painted pictures of celebrities. He died on 22nd February, 1987.

279. ROBERT FRANK

Swiss photographer and filmmaker Robert Frank was born on 9th November, 1924. He grew up under the World War II threat of Nazism. This gave him an understanding of oppression and suffering, which made him turn to photography as a creative outlet. In 1947, he migrated to USA and moved to New York, where he pursued a career in photography. He is widely known for his 1958 photography book, *The Americans*, which provides an outsider's view of American society.

280. FREDERIC AUGUSTE BARTHOLDI

Frederic Auguste Bartholdi was a French sculptor, his most well-known work being the Statue of Liberty in the USA. Bartholdi was born on 2nd April, 1834, in Alsace, France. At the age of 20, he travelled to Egypt and studied Egyptian art. He was very impressed by the colossal monuments and they helped to shape up his artistic vision. He began working on the Statue of Liberty after 1875.

It is widely believed that he modelled Lady Liberty's face after his mother. He died of tuberculosis on 4th October, 1904, in Paris.

281. PAUL CEZANNE

Paul Cezanne was a French artist and painter, whose work led the change that art went through from the 19th to the 20th century. He was born on 19th January, 1839. Cezanne can be said to form the bridge between the dominant style of art in the 19th century (impressionism) and the movement that swept through the 20th century (cubism). Both Henri Matisse and Pablo Picasso, great cubist painters, were highly influenced by Cezanne. He died on 22nd October, 1906.

282. CLAUDE MONET

Claude Monet was a French painter, who founded the Impressionist Movement. He was born on 14th November, 1840, in Paris. He enjoyed drawing ever since he was a child. He started by drawing very impressive caricatures of people.

He scribbled caricatures of his teachers in his schoolbooks and by 15, he had gained a reputation as a caricature artist. His work was displayed at a local frame maker's shop. People soon began recognising their friends and acquaintances in the drawings. It was not long before he started charging people to draw their caricatures and this gave him a steady income.

Monet became known as an "Impressionist"—a title derived from his painting, *Impression, Sunrise*. The brush strokes were lively and spontaneous, capturing the feeling of the moment.

Monet was one of the first artists to paint outdoors. Though paintings of landscapes were common, they were almost always painted from recollection in a studio and never a direct impression. Monet died on 5th December, 1926.

Impressionism was a form of art characterised by small, thin, yet visible strokes. Impressionists believed in capturing the essence of the subject instead of the detail.

283. AUGUSTE RODIN

Auguste Rodin was a well-known French sculptor, considered by some to be the greatest portraitist in history. He worked on both bronze and marble to create his sculptures. He was born on 12th November, 1840, into a poor family. He enrolled in an art school at the age of 13. He tried to get admission in the École des Beaux-Arts, but failed the competitive exam thrice. He decided to earn a living by doing decorative stonework.

By the time he was 35, he had not yet found a personally expressive style because of the pressures of decorative work. In 1875, he travelled to Italy, where he visited Genoa, Florence, Rome, Naples and Venice, and was inspired by great artists like Michelangelo and Donatello.

Under their influence, he moulded his first famous bronze sculpture, *The Vanquished*. It was so realistic that people accused him of taking the mould of an actual person!

He established his identity as an exemplary sculptor only at the age of 40. He died on 17th November, 1917.

Rodin's last work, *The Gates of Hell*, remained unfinished because of his death, but he remained popular for his most well-known sculptures—*The Thinker* and *The Kiss*.

284. PIERRE-AUGUSTE RENOIR

French impressionist artist Pierre-Auguste Renoir was born on 25th February, 1841, in Limoges, France. His artistic talent was evident even when he was a little boy, when he worked as an apprentice to a porcelain painter. In 1862, Renoir began studying art in Paris. There, he met some fellow-painters along with whom he would launch the Impressionism Art movement.

Renoir died on 3rd December, 1919, in Cagnes-sur-Mer, France. The warm sensuality that his paintings exuded made him one of the most celebrated modern artists.

285. ANTONI GAUDI

Antoni Gaudi was a revolutionary Spanish architect. He was born on 25th June, 1852. He developed a keen interest in architecture at a young age. He went to school in Barcelona, the city that inspired many of his great works. Gaudi was part of the Catalan Modernista movement. The building that Antoni Gaudi is best known for, though, is La Sagrada Familia in Barcelona. He began making this huge church in 1882 and he worked on it until he died on 10th June, 1926. Sadly, it has been left unfinished.

286. VINCENT VAN GOGH

Vincent Van Gogh was a Dutch painter, who is one of the greatest post-impressionist painters. He was born on 30th March, 1853, in Netherlands.

His work was a major influence on 20th century art. He struggled with psychological illnesses and was poor throughout his life. He was also virtually unrecognised throughout his life.

At 16, he apprenticed with a branch of art dealers. Dealing with art on a daily basis aroused an artistic sensibility in him and he soon began to admire Dutch masters like Rembrandt. He later tried his hand at many professions, including teaching and he even tried joining the Church. However, he was thrown out of the church and took to painting after that.

His paintings became popular only after his death. They were characterised by bright colours, deliberate brush strokes and forced forms. His painting, *The Starry Night*, has become one of the most celebrated art masterpieces of all time.

Van Gogh pioneered the art movement that came to be known as "Expressionism". He died in France on 29th July, 1890, from a self-inflicted gunshot wound.

Van Gogh was known to be mentally disturbed. In 1888, he cut off a part of his ear with a razor blade when Gauguin, a painter who was living with him, announced that he wanted to leave.

287. GUSTAV KLIMT

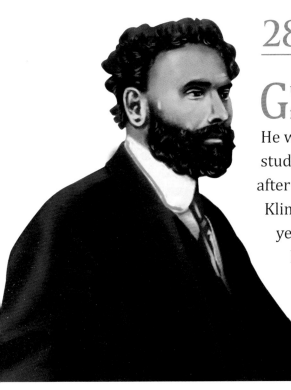

Gustav Klimt was an Austrian painter and founder of the school called Vienna Sezession. He was born in Austria on 14th July, 1862. He studied at the Vienna School of Decorative Arts, after which he opened an independent studio. Klimt painted many images of women during his years with the Vienna. He also painted many landscapes. In the 1890s, he began taking yearly vacations to the Austrian lake, Attersee, with a female acquaintance and her family. It was this area that inspired his landscapes. He died on 6th February, 1918.

288. EDVARD MUNCH

Edvard Munch was a Norwegian painter, who greatly influenced German expressionism. He was born on 12th December, 1863, in Löten, Norway. He began to pursue a career in engineering, but abandoned it and decided to devote his life to painting. He established a style of painting that was free flowing. His painting reflected his internal emotions and was like nothing anyone had ever seen before. His painting, *The Scream* is possibly the most recognisable works in the history of art. His later works were not as intense as his earlier works, but his legacy was already established. He died on 23rd January, 1944.

289. ALEXANDER BOGOMAZOV

Alexander or Oleksandr Bogomazov was a Ukrainian painter. He was born on 7th April, 1880. He was a part of Russian Avant-garde movement. He wrote a treatise in 1914 called *The Art of Painting and the Elements* in which he analysed the relationship between the object, artist, picture and spectator. It is the basis of modern art. He attended the Institute of Agriculture in Kherson for six years. After that, he went to the Kiev Art School for another three years. Though he mastered many art styles, he was most famous for his cubo-futurism and spectralism. He died on 3rd June, 1930.

290. FRANZ MARC

Franz Marc was a German painter. He was born on 8th February, 1880, in Munich. He was the second son of painter Wilhelm Marc. He was part of a huge movement in the arts called German expressionism. This movement believed that art must be a reflection of the artist's feelings and emotions instead of imitating nature or illustrating a literary theme. For the first time in history, art was being created out of an inner necessity on the part of the artist to create it. Franz Marc is known for his mystic paintings of animals. He died on 4th March, 1916.

291. PABLO PICASSO

Pablo Picasso was one of the greatest artists of the 20th century and also one of the pioneers of the cubism art form. He was born on 25th October, 1881, in Malaga, Spain. His father was an art teacher and this helped cultivate Picasso's interest. His father began tutoring him in art from the age of seven. Picasso kept practising until he was an even better artist than his father.

At the age of 16, Picasso started attending Madrid's Royal Academy of San Fernand. When he went to Paris in 1900, Picasso's art attracted the attention of several art collectors, including the famous Gertrude Stein. 1907 marked the year that Picasso created *Les Demoiselles d'Avignon*, which laid the foundation for the cubism art movement. Cubism involves breaking up the painting's subject and re-assembling it on the canvas in an abstract composition.

Some of his famous paintings include *The Old Guitarist, Asleep and Seated Woman* and *Guernica*, a mural about the Spanish Civil War. Pablo Picasso died on 8th April, 1973, in Mougins, France.

Pablo Picasso's full name has 22 words! He was baptised as Pablo Diego José Francisco de Paula Juan Nepomuceno María de los Remedios Cipriano de la Santísima Trinidad Martyr Patricio Clito Ruíz y Picasso. He was named after several saints and relatives.

292. TITIAN

Titian is the English name of Tiziano Vecellio, a 16th century oil painter who was born between 1488 and 1490 in Venice, Italy. He rose to fame at an early age for being a supreme painter. Highly respected, his peers called him the "Sun amidst small stars".

In his early years, he studied under the popular painters, Gentile and Giovanni Bellini. He learnt a lot from his contemporaries, too. Titian grew to be the best painter in Venice and had great influence over western art.

Titian's work used clean colours and portrayed an idealistic beauty, both in nature and in people. He was one of the first painters to use quick underpaintings rather than elaborate underdrawings for his art. He contributed significantly to all the major areas of Renaissance art.

He was appointed as the official painter to the Republic in 1516. Towards the end of his life, Titian abandoned the rules and painted more emotionally.

His life came to an end on 27th August, 1576, when he passed away from the plague.

Titian was Venice's only plague victim to get a church burial. Owing to their large numbers, the other victims were unceremoniously buried in mass graves.

293. HENRI CARTIER-BRESSON

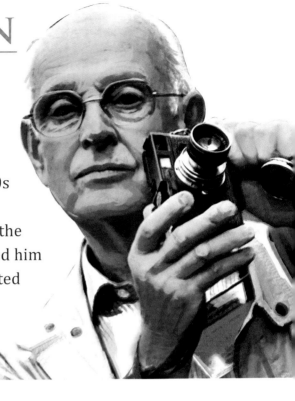

Henri Cartier-Bresson was a French photographer, who helped establish photojournalism as a form of art. He was born on 22nd August, 1908. He had a lustrous career, covering famous events from the 1930s to the 1970s. He covered many of the world's biggest events, from the Spanish Civil War to the French uprisings in 1968. His work has earned him the title, "Father of Photojournalism". He started taking photographs in the 1930s and was already holding his first exhibitions and publications by 1933. He died on 3rd August, 2004.

294. JACKSON POLLOCK

Paul Jackson Pollock was an American painter known for his involvement in the Abstract Expressionist Movement. He was born on 28th January, 1912. He gained fame during his lifetime itself. He was first exposed to liquid paint at a workshop in New York City held by Mexican muralist, David Alfaro Siqueiros in 1936. Later, paint pouring was one of several techniques he used on canvases in the early 1940s. Some of his famous work includes *Male and Female* and *Composition with Pouring I*. He died on 11th August, 1956.

295. ÉDOUARD MANET

Born into a middle-class family in Paris on 23rd January, 1832, Édouard Manet was always artistically inclined. His parents wished for him to pursue a more traditional career, but he defied them and went to art school instead.

One of Manet's hobbies was to sneak away from home and go to the Louvre museum. He would sit there for hours and try to copy the displayed masterpieces. For three years, Manet travelled across Europe and learnt about many brilliant painters.

After six years of study, Manet opened his own art studio. His painting, *The Absinthe Drinker*, is considered a prime example of the realism art form even today.

However, Manet's art is significant because it encapsulates the shift in the art scene from realism to impressionism. Manet's other famous works include *The Luncheon on the Grass* and *Olympia*. He died on 30th April, 1883, in Paris, by which time he was already considered a path-breaking artist.

Manet liked to paint regular people doing everyday activities. He painted beggars, singers and people from the streets of Paris.

296. RAVI VARMA

Raja Ravi Varma, born on 29th April, 1848, in Kerala, India, is an Indian painter who is famously known for his work of amalgamating Hindu mythology with European realist historicist painting style. He was one of the first Indian artists to use oil paints and master the art of lithographic reproduction of his work. He was also the first Indian to acclimatise Indian subjects, styles and themes using western techniques. In 1873, he won the Governor's Gold Medal for the painting *Nair Lady Adorning* Her Hair. He died on 2nd October, 1906.

297. FRANK GEHRY

Frank Gehry is a Canadian-American architect. He was born on 28th February, 1929. He studied at the University of Southern California and Harvard University. He is renowned for his bold, post-modern architecture and unusual creations. His most famous works include the Walt Disney Concert Hall in Los Angeles and the Guggenheim Museum in Bilbao. He has also won many awards, some of which are the Pritzker Architecture Prize (1989), the National Medal of the Arts (1998) and the American Institute of Architects Gold Medal (1999).

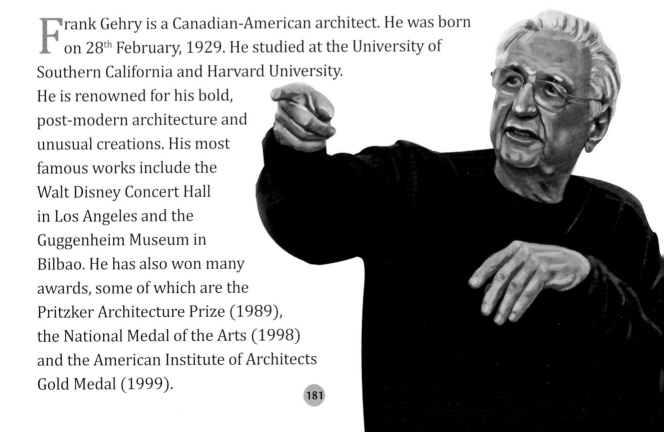

Mesmerising Musicians

This section focusses on people who have made significant contributions in the field of music. Let's find out about their talents and contributions as well as about their lives. Let's see how their music has influenced people all over the world. Read on and get to know more about these mesmerising musicians.

298. MICHAEL JACKSON

Michael Joseph Jackson was an American singer, songwriter, dancer and philanthropist, who is called the "King of Pop". He was born on 29th August, 1958, in Gary, Indiana. He began his career with four of his brothers, forming the famous band, the "Jackson 5".

In 1968, when Jackson was only 10, Motown records signed the Jackson 5. They toured internationally, releasing six more albums between 1976 and 1984. After their success, Jackson decided to become a solo act. His debut album was *Got to be there*, which was released on 24th January, 1972.

Jackson has been inducted into the Rock and Roll Hall of Fame twice. He has eight Guinness World Records throughout his successful musical career. He passed away on 25th June, 2009.

299. THE BEATLES

In the 1960s, a band from Liverpool, England, burst into the pop music scene and changed it forever. "The Beatles" comprised of George Harrison, John Lennon, Paul McCartney and Ringo Starr. Paul McCartney and John Lennon formed the nucleus of the group.

All the members of the band were united by a mutual love and respect for American rock and roll. They did several small-time gigs in Liverpool and Hamburg before they were spotted by Brian Epstein, a local record store owner. He was convinced of their commercial potential and he became their manager. He finally got them a contract with Parlophone, a subsidiary of the giant EMI label. The Beatles soon shot to fame in the UK as well as internationally.

The Beatles were also the leaders of the "counterculture" that swept the world in the 1960s. Their songs were known for their anti-war, anti-capitalist stance. They were openly against the Vietnam War and John Lennon was nearly deported because of it.

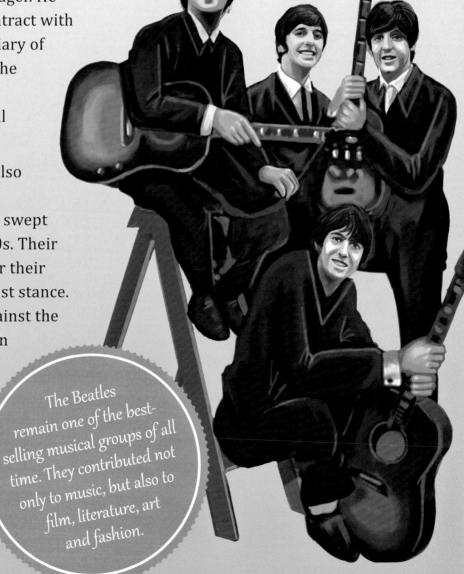

The Beatles remain one of the best-selling musical groups of all time. They contributed not only to music, but also to film, literature, art and fashion.

300. LOUIS ARMSTRONG

Louis Armstrong, also known as "Satchmo" and "Pops", is one of the pillars of jazz music. He was born on 4th August, 1901, in New Orleans, USA. In a career spanning nearly 50 years, Armstrong gained popularity as an iconic jazz musician. His skill with the trumpet and his trademark gruff voice made him the star attraction at concerts.

He was one of the first African-American musicians to overcome racial discrimination in 1920s America. He paved the way for many other musicians. He died in New York on 6th July, 1971.

301. FRANK SINATRA

Frank Sinatra was born in Hoboken, New Jersey, USA, on 12th December, 1915. His deep, soulful voice brought him great success singing big band songs in the 1940s and 1950s.

After delivering hit song after hit song, he went on to act in a number of films and even won an Oscar for the film *From Here to Eternity*. He also received 11 Grammy Awards during his lifetime. He died at the age of 82 on 14th May, 1998.

302. MILES DAVIS

Miles Dewey Davis was not only a famous American jazz musician, but also one of the most influential musicians of the 20th century. He was born in Illinois, USA, on 26th May, 1926. He was only 16 when he started his career. He has led several major developments in music, including bebop, cool jazz, hard bop, modal jazz and jazz fusion. His record debut came in 1946.

303. JOHNNY CASH

Johnny Cash was born on 26th February, 1932, in Arkansas, USA. He showed a passion for music from an early age, having picked up the guitar when he was 12. As a young man, Cash joined the US Air Force and was sent to Germany, where he formed a band called "The Landsberg Barbarians" with some Air Force friends. His 1957 song, *I Walk The Line,* shot to No.1 and catapulted Cash to fame. He went on to write many hit songs with his wife, June Carter. Cash died on 12th September, 2003 at Nashville, Tennessee, USA.

304. JAMES BROWN

James Brown was fondly known as the "Godfather of Soul". He was born on 3rd May, 1933. He was so poor that he was sent away from school for "insufficient clothes". He also went to prison at a young age.

In 1955, he was invited to join an R&B vocal group. With his leadership skills and great talent, Brown quickly became the leader of the group. They changed their name to the "Famous Flames" and started performing secular music at nightclubs.

In 1956, the Famous Flames recorded a demo tape of the song *Please, Please, Please*, which impressed a talent scout for King Records. Soon, the song had reached No. 1 on the charts.

James Brown had a very versatile voice. He could croon soulfully and "scream" in perfect key, all in the same song!

That was just the beginning for Brown. He went on to record many popular songs during his career that spanned six decades.

His legacy came to an end on 25th December, 2006, when he breathed his last in Atlanta, Georgia, USA.

305. ELVIS PRESLEY

Known as the King of Rock and Roll, Elvis Presley was born on 8th January, 1935, in Mississippi, USA. He came from very humble beginnings and grew to become the biggest music icon of his time. He appeared in 33 successful films, several television appearances and found great acclaim through his record-breaking live concerts. He is one of the highest-selling musicians of all time and has won gold, platinum and multi-platinum awards. Also under his belt are three Grammy Awards and the Grammy Lifetime Achievement Award, which he won at the age of 36. He died on 16th August, 1977.

306. PAVAROTTI

Luciano Pavarotti was an opera singer, who helped to make opera more popular in mainstream music. He was born on 12th October, 1935, in Italy. When he was 19 years old, Pavarotti started training to become a professional opera singer. Seeing his talent, the tutor offered to teach him for free! In 1966, he became the first ever opera singer to be able to hit all nine "high Cs". This made him a global phenomenon. He died on 6th September, 2007.

307. BOB DYLAN

Bob Dylan is an American musician, singer-songwriter, artist and writer. He was born as Robert Allen Zimmerman on 24th May, 1941. He adopted the name "Bob Dylan" while he performed folk and country songs as a college student. His thought-provoking lyrics filled with social, political and literary undertones led people to refer to him as the Shakespeare of his generation. His most famous work dates back to the 1960s, but he has remained an influential figure in pop music. He released his latest album in 2012 and continues to tour all around the world.

308. JOHN LENNON

John Lennon was the lead singer, guitarist and song writer of the iconic musical group, "The Beatles". He was born on 9th October, 1940, in Liverpool, England. He met Paul McCartney in 1957 and invited McCartney to join his music group. They eventually formed the most successful songwriting partnership in musical history. Lennon left The Beatles in 1969 and later released albums with his wife, Yoko Ono. He was heavily involved with social activism, which reflected in his music. A mentally unstable fan assassinated Lennon on 8th December, 1980, in New York, USA.

309. JIMI HENDRIX

Guitarist, singer and songwriter Jimi Hendrix was born Johnny Allen Hendrix on 27th November, 1942. Even though his career lasted only four years, he completely redefined rock music in that time. Inspired by Elvis Presley, Hendrix mastered the electric guitar and moved to London, where he formed a band called "The Jimi Hendrix Experience". The band soon had three hit singles—*Hey Joe*, *The Wind Cries Mary* and *Purple Haze*. Their two albums were also successes. Hendrix was legendary because he blurred the lines between musical genres. He died on 18th September, 1970, at the height of his fame.

310. JIM MORRISON

Jim Morrison was an iconic rock musician and the lead singer of the band, "The Doors". He was born on 8th December, 1943, at Florida, USA. The Doors shot into fame overnight when their single, *Light My Fire*, topped the Billboard Hot 100 Singles Chart. Morrison was very intellectual and liked to read. The songs he wrote with band mate Robby Krieger had meaningful, poetic lyrics. In 1971, Morrison left the band and moved to Paris to write poetry. On 3rd July of the same year, he was found dead. He was just 27.

311. BOB MARLEY

Bob Marley has gone down in history for bringing Jamaican reggae music to international ears. He was born in Nine Mile, Saint Ann, Jamaica, on 6th February, 1945. It all started in 1963, when Marley and his friends formed a band called "The Wailers". Through the course of his career, Marley went on to sell more than 20 million records. He was the first superstar to emerge from a so-called backward country. Marley inspired people not just with his music, but also with his Rastafarian beliefs. He died in Miami, Florida, on 11th May, 1981.

312. FREDDIE MERCURY

Freddie Mercury was the lead singer and songwriter for the world-famous rock band "Queen". His real name was Farookh Bulsara and he was born on 5th September, 1946, in Zanzibar, Tanzania. He was originally from India. He studied in a boarding school there, which is where he learnt the piano. He then attended London's Ealing College of Art. As a singer, he had a very impressive vocal range. His unmistakable vocals gave Queen classic hits like *Bohemian Rhapsody* and *Under Pressure*. He passed away on 24th November, 1991.

313. DAVID BOWIE

In the 1970s, when he was at his peak, David Bowie was known as the master of reinvention because of his ever-changing music and appearance. He was born David Robert Jones in Brixton, South London, England, on 8th January, 1947. He joined six different musical groups, but none of them did well. It was only after embracing his love for theatricals and his eccentric personality that he soared to superstardom. In 1996, he was inducted into the Rock and Roll Hall of Fame. He last released an album in 2013 after a 10-year hiatus.

314. ELTON JOHN

Sir Elton John is one of the most celebrated British musicians of all time. Born as Reginald Kenneth Dwight, he was a child prodigy with a natural talent for the piano. He was born on 25th March, 1947. After hearing a melody, he could play it by the ear! Among other awards and accolades, he has won six Grammy Awards, an Academy Award, a Golden Globe Award and a Tony Award. In 1998, the Queen of England knighted John for his contribution to music and charity.

315. YANNI

Yanni is the stage name of Yiannis Chryssomallis, a Greek-born American pianist, keyboardist, composer and music producer. Born on 14th November, 1954, he is credited with popularising New Age instrumental music. Yanni's albums have repeatedly topped the Billboard charts in the "Top New Age Album" category and he has sold more than 20 million records. He is also known for his live concert performances and has performed at iconic sites like the Burj Khalifa in Dubai, the Taj Mahal in India and the Kremlin in Russia.

316. JOHANN SEBASTIAN BACH

Johann Sebastian Bach was a famous German music composer. He was born on 21st March, 1685, into a family of musicians. He is best known for his compositions on the organ. Some even call him the best organ player of all time. He was orphaned at the age of nine, after which he went to live with his brother, an organ player. Bach followed in his brother's footsteps and started playing for the Church in his town.

In 1723, he was appointed as the music director of the Thomasschule. Here, he was in great demand because of his immense knowledge and talent. He even began publishing his own work. Though he wrote more than 300 musical pieces, he always enjoyed studying music and playing instruments more than writing. He died on 28th July, 1750.

317. MADONNA

Madonna is often referred to as the "Queen of Pop". Born on 16th August, 1958, in Michigan, USA, she moved to New York City to become a dancer. But fate had different plans for her. She got signed on by Sire Records and released her first music album at the age of 24.

She continued to rule the pop music scene throughout the 1990s and 2000s. Many of her hits topped the charts at No. 1. Some of these are *Papa Don't Preach, Like a Prayer, Frozen* and *4 Minutes*.

Madonna is known to constantly re-invent herself and pleasantly surprise her audience. She has dabbled in dancing, acting, dancing and writing. Madonna even started her own entertainment company called "Maverick Entertainment".

She was inducted into the Rock and Roll Hall of Fame in 2008. In that same year, she was ranked second on the Billboard Hot 100 All-Time Top Artists. In 2013, Forbes magazine named her the fifth most powerful celebrity and also the highest-earning one.

In 2003, Madonna wrote a children's book called *The English Roses*. Not only did it top the New York Times Best Seller list, but it also became the fastest-selling children's picture book of all time!

318. MOZART

Wolfgang Amadeus Mozart was a child prodigy and one of the most famous musicians of all time. He was born in Salzburg, Austria on 27th January, 1756. His father, Leopold Mozart, was a choir master. At the young age of four, he began keyboard lessons and started performing flawlessly. By age five, he was composing short pieces by himself. At the age of eight, this child prodigy published his first two sonatas. His skills as a composer continued to develop and by the age of 13, he had composed his first opera. Mozart passed away on 5th December, 1791, leaving behind a collection of more than 600 compositions.

319. BEETHOVEN

Ludwig van Beethoven was one of the world's greatest music composers. He was born in Bonn, Germany, in 1770. He wrote many symphonies, tones and pieces for music, using instruments such as the piano, organ and violin. He learned all these instruments by the young age of eight and wrote his first composition when he was only 11. He had a hearing problem which kept getting worse as he aged. Amazingly, he composed his most significant work when he was completely deaf! He died on 26th March, 1827, at Vienna, Austria.

320. THE ROLLING STONES

The Rolling Stones is an English rock band that is credited with making blues a major part of rock and roll. It was formed in 1962 and originally consisted of Brian Jones (guitar, harmonica), Ian Stewart (piano), Mick Jagger (lead vocals, harmonica), Keith Richards (guitar), Bill Wyman (bass) and Charlie Watts (drums). Though a lot of the members have been replaced, the band is still active and celebrated its 50th anniversary in 2012. The Rolling Stones were inducted into the Rock and Roll Hall of Fame in 1989 and the UK Music Hall of Fame in 2004. "Rolling Stone" magazine ranked them fourth on the "100 Greatest Artists of All Time" list.

321. PINK FLOYD

Pink Floyd was an English rock band that was formed in 1967. Syd Barrett, Roger Waters, Nick Mason and Richard Wright were the founding members. Step Gilmour joined the band in 1968 and in the following year, Barrett quit the band because of health reasons. They earned laurels for their unique sound, thought-provoking lyrics, quirky cover art on their albums and their flamboyant live shows. Pink Floyd has sold over 200 million albums worldwide. They officially disbanded in 2006, bringing a four-decade legacy to an end.

322. KURT COBAIN

Kurt Cobain was an American musician and artist, best known as the lead singer, guitarist and songwriter of the rock band "Nirvana". Born on 20th February, 1967, Cobain formed Nirvana in 1987. After signing with major label DGC Records, the band found breakthrough success with *Smells Like Teen Spirit* from its 1991 album "Nevermind".

Nirvana is said to be the pioneer of the grunge rock music genre and has sold over 75 million records worldwide. Cobain passed away on 5th April, 1994, from a self-inflicted gunshot wound, when he was just 27 years old.

323. THE EAGLES

The Eagles are an American band that pioneered the country rock genre of music, blending two of America's most-loved music genres. Formed in 1971, The Eagles consists of Glenn Frey, Don Henley, Bernie Leadon, Randy Meisner and later, Timothy Schmit. Seven of their songs and six albums made it to No.1. Their album "Hotel California" is ranked 37th on Rolling Stone's "Greatest Albums of All Time" list.

324. ABBA

ABBA was a Swedish pop group formed in Stockholm in 1972. The name was coined with the first letters of the members' names—Agnetha Faltskog, Bjorn Ulvaeus, Benny Andersson and Anni-Frid Lyngstad. They became the first musicians from mainland Europe to break into the British, American and Australian pop charts. "ABBA" put Sweden on the global music map and helped pave the way for other European musicians.

They topped the worldwide music charts throughout the 1970s. In 1974, they represented Sweden at the Eurovision Song Contest and won Sweden its first ever victory in the contest. On the contest's 50th anniversary in 2005, ABBA was felicitated again. Their song *Waterloo* was chosen as the best song in the history of the Eurovision contest. ABBA's worldwide sales were about 300–400 million. This makes them one of the highest-selling bands of all time, second only to The Beatles.

In 2008, the musical *Mamma Mia!* was adapted into a film starring Meryl Streep. It went on to become the most successful film in the UK for that year.

325. EMINEM

Eminem is the stage name of Marshall Bruce Mathers III, one of the most famous modern rap artists. He was born on 17th October, 1972. Eminem started rapping at the age of 14 with his high school friends. His style slowly developed to include an alter-ego called "Slim Shady". Eminem's uniqueness caught the eye of rap icon, Dr. Dre. He released his first album, *The Slim Shady LP*, in 1999. Apart from his solo act, he is also part of the groups "D12" and "Bad Meets Evil".

326. A. R. RAHMAN

Allah Rakha Rahman, more commonly known as A. R. Rahman, is an Indian singer and music composer. His brilliant work has earned him the title "Mozart of Madras". Rahman began studying the piano when he was just four years old. By the time he was 11 years old, he dropped out of school and started playing the piano professionally.

Rahman is notable for his work on films like *Roja*, *Lagaan* and his international breakthrough, *Slumdog Millionaire*.

Rahman won the Academy Award for best song for *Jai Ho* from *Slumdog Millionaire*. He has also won Grammys, a Golden Globe and a BAFTA for his work on *Slumdog Millionaire*.

Fantastic Food Lords

This section focusses on people who have laid out the ingredients for modern cooking. Their work has majorly contributed to shaping the culinary world. Let's find out about their inventions and discoveries as well as about their lives. Read on and get to know these fantastic foodies.

327. JAMIE OLIVER

Jamie Oliver is a British chef, restaurateur, cookbook writer and media personality. He was born on 27th May, 1975. Though he is proficient in many cuisines, his specialty is Italian food. His focus is on improving unhealthy diets and poor cooking habits in the USA and UK.

His parents ran a pub called "The Cricketer" in Essex, where he first tried his hand at cooking. He was working at "The River Cafe" as a sous chef in 1997, when he was noticed by BBC while they were making a documentary on the cafe.

Today, Jamie Oliver boasts of having prepared lunch for the Prime Minister at the time, Tony Blair, and having starred in several shows.

328. BARTOLOMEO SCAPPI

Bartolomeo Scappi was a famous Renaissance chef. He was born around 1500. Recent research shows that he was born in Dumenza in Lombardi. He is known for the lavish banquets that he cooked for the Popes. He cooked for a total of six popes throughout his career. In fact, while Michelangelo was painting the ceiling of the Sistine Chapel, Scappi was cooking in the kitchen! He even cooked for the likes of Holy Roman Emperor Charles V and Pope Paul III.

In 1570, he published a book *Opera dell'arte del cucinare,* which listed 1,000 renaissance recipes, cooking techniques and tools. It also contains the first known image of a fork. The *Opera dell'arte del cucinare* was translated into English in 2008 by the food historian, Terence Scully. Scappi died on 13th April, 1577.

329. JOHN MONTAGU

John Montagu is credited with inventing the sandwich. He was born on 13th November, 1718, in Chiswick, England. He inherited the title Earl of Sandwich and joined Parliament. A popular story says that the Earl was such an ardent gambler that he had no time to eat meals while he was playing. He would often ask his servants to get him slices of meat between two slices of bread. This allowed him to eat a meal without stopping the card game! Since he was the "Earl of Sandwich", people soon started asking for the same as "Sandwich". And voila! The sandwich was born. He died on 30th April, 1792.

330. HENRI NESTLÉ

Henri Nestlé was a Swiss confectioner who founded Nestlé, the world's largest food and beverage company. He was born as Heinrich Nestlé on 10th August, 1814, in Frankfurt, Germany. He is also credited with inventing condensed milk. In 1843, he bought a company that produced rapeseeds. He soon expanded to produce oil lamps, liqueurs, rum, absinthe and vinegar. By 1867, he was producing baby formula, a powdered milk product, which was a substitute for breast milk. People soon recognised the value of this and the product became very popular. He died on 7th July, 1890.

331. GEORGE CRUM

George Crum is the man who is thought to have invented the potato crisp. He was born in 1822. Crum owned a small lakeside café. The story goes that a customer once sent his French fries back to the kitchen, saying that they were too thick. Crum, who was known to be sarcastic and irritable, cut the potato as thin as he could, fried it in grease and sent them back to the customer. To his surprise, the guest actually enjoyed the crispy fried potato and asked for some more. Soon, other guests began asking for them as well and before he knew it, the potato crisp had been invented. He died on 22nd July, 1914.

332. MILTON HERSHEY

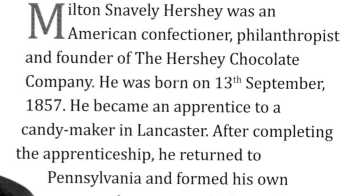

Milton Snavely Hershey was an American confectioner, philanthropist and founder of The Hershey Chocolate Company. He was born on 13th September, 1857. He became an apprentice to a candy-maker in Lancaster. After completing the apprenticeship, he returned to Pennsylvania and formed his own caramel company, which soon became very popular. In fact, the town in which the factory stood came to be known as Hershey! He died on 13th October, 1945.

333. JOHN STITH PEMBERTON

John Stith Pemberton is best known as the inventor of Coca Cola. He was born on 8th January, 1831. He was a Colonel in the Confederate army and was wounded during the war. After this, he got addicted to morphine. As a pharmacist, he tried to find a cure to counteract his addiction. He experimented with coca and the popular "coca cola" was born. But soon after its invention, he went bankrupt and sold the rights to Asa Candler. He died on 16th August, 1888.

334. JAMES BEARD

Beard was an American chef and food writer. He was born on 5ᵗʰ May, 1903, in Oregan, USA. He inherited his love for food from his mother. He was responsible for establishing a gourmet American food identity. He had a quirky personality and introduced French cooking to the American middle and upper classes in the 1950s.

He wrote an incredible amount of literature throughout his life, including 20 books. He also has a foundation of his own, which hosts the "Beard Awards" annually in many culinary genres.

He first tried his hand at theatre, which did not go very well. So, he opened a catering company in the late 1930s.

He published books containing all his recipes, called *Hors D'Oeuvre* and *Canapés*.

He was also one of the first people to host television cooking shows. He inspired the likes of Julia Child and many other chefs. He died on 21ˢᵗ January, 1985.

At the age of three, James Beard suffered from malaria. This gave him some time to enjoy his mother's cooking.

335. RUTH WAKEFIELD

Ruth Wakefield is the woman responsible for chocolate chip cookies! She was born on 17th June, 1903. She graduated from the Framingham State Normal School Department of Household Arts in 1924. After this, she became a dietician and food lecturer. The invention of chocolate chip cookies was actually an accident. She owned an inn. One day, while baking cookies, she ran out of baker's chocolate. So, she substituted it with pieces of Nestle's chocolate. The guests loved the cookies and chocolate chip cookies were born! She died on 10th January, 1977.

336. JULIA CHILD

Julia Carolyn Child was an American chef, author and television personality. She was born on 15th August, 1912. She moved to France in 1948, where she developed a keen liking for French cuisine. She wanted to adapt sophisticated French cuisine to suit the average American. With this purpose, she published her debut cookbook, *Mastering the Art of French Cooking*, which was famous for introducing French cooking to the American public. She also anchored several television shows, the most notable of which was "The French Chef". She died on 13th August, 2004.

337. IRVINE ROBBINS AND BURTON BASKIN

Irvine "Irv" Robbins and Burton "Burt" Baskin were brothers-in-law, who founded the famous ice-cream franchise, Baskin Robbins. Irvine was born on 6th December, 1917, in Manitoba, Canada. Burt was born on 17th December, 1913 in Streator, Illinois, USA.

The two men wished to create an innovative ice cream store that could also serve as a neighbourhood gathering place for families. Both Irvine "Irv" Robbins and Burton "Burt" Baskin loved old fashioned ice-cream and wanted to provide their customers with a large variety of flavours.

Taking Irv's father's advice, both of them started out separately. In 1945, Irv opened Snowbird Ice Cream in Glendale, California. His store featured 21 flavours and emphasised high-quality ice cream sold in a fun, personalised atmosphere.

A year later, Burt opened Burton's Ice Cream Shop in Pasadena, California. By 1948, they had six stores between them. Their concept eventually grew into Baskin-Robbins.

The company has introduced more than 1,000 flavours since 1945.

338. WOLFGANG PUCK

Wolfgang Puck is an Austrian celebrity chef, restaurateur, businessman and he occasionally even acts! He was born as Wolfgang Johannes Topfschnig on 8th July, 1949. His father abandoned his mother before Wolfgang was born. His mother later remarried a man named Joseph Puck, who adopted and raised Wolfgang.

Wolfgang learned how to cook from his mother, who sometimes worked as a pastry chef. He trained as an apprentice under Raymond Thuilier in Paris. He then moved to the USA in 1973. He became a chef and part owner at the restaurant "Ma Maison".

He published his first cookbook *Modern French Cooking for the American Kitchen* in 1981. It was a great success and he opened the well-known restaurant Spago in Beverly Hills. It has been in the list of top 40 restaurants in the USA since 2004.

He also owns the group "Wolfgang Puck Companies", which includes the Wolfgang Puck Fine Dining Group, Wolfgang Puck Worldwide, Inc. and Wolfgang Puck Catering.

Puck operates with a signature form-to-table philosophy — all his food ingredients are produced locally!

339. THOMAS KELLER

Thomas Keller is an American chef, restaurateur and cookbook writer. He was born on 14th October, 1955. He is known for his culinary skill as well as the ability to establish a restaurant that is relaxing and exciting at the same time. Keller found his calling when he began working at a restaurant owned by his mother. He moved to France in 1983. He worked at many renowned Michelin-starred restaurants including Guy Savoy and Taillevent. He opened his first restaurant, Rakel, in New York City in 1986.

340. ALAIN DUCASSE

Alain Ducasse is easily one of the moguls of the restaurant industry. He was born on 13th September, 1956. He's been in the business for several decades and has several restaurants to his name – even a group of restaurants that deal with everything from actual restaurant operations to consultancy to cooking schools and beyond. When people say that the sky is the limit, it is meant figuratively. Ducasse, however, seems to have taken it literally. In partnership with the European Space Agency, Ducasse is actually sending food into space!

341. ANTHONY BOURDAIN

Anthony Michael Bourdain is an American chef, author and television personality. He was born on 25th June, 1956. His interest in food was sparked when, as a young boy, he ate an oyster in France. He graduated from the Culinary Institute of America. He started as a dishwasher and gradually climbed the ladder of success to become executive chef. He is famous for a book he wrote in 2000, *Kitchen Confidential: Adventures in the Culinary Underbelly*. But he is best known as the host of the 2005 Travel Channel's food and culture shows, "Anthony Bourdain: No Reservations" and "The Layover". He joined CNN to host "Anthony Bourdain: Parts Unknown" in 2013.

342. NIGELLA LAWSON

Nigella Lawson is an English journalist, broadcaster, television personality, gourmet and food writer. She was born on 6th January, 1960, in London, UK. Her family owned the J. Lyons and Co. food and catering business. She eventually decided to take up a career in publishing. She wrote books like *How to Eat*, which is immensely popular. She is also known for her work on television shows like "Nigella Bites" and "The Taste".

343. GORDON RAMSAY

Gordon Ramsay is an American chef and TV personality, who is well-known for his temper and raging outbursts in the kitchen. However, he is still one of the best chefs in the world and has several successful restaurants to prove it. He was born on 8th November, 1966, in Scotland. Ramsay actually wanted to pursue a career in professional soccer. Unfortunately, he suffered from a knee injury, which put an end to his dream.

He then enrolled in a hotel management school. After graduating, he apprenticed with Marco Pierre White at Harvey's in London. In 1993, Ramsay took the reins of the newly opened Aubergine. Within three years, he had earned two Michelin stars.

In 1998, he opened Gordon Ramsay's. The London restaurant was quickly recognised as one of the best in the world and was awarded three stars by Michelin. Today, he is best known for his role in competitive cooking shows like MasterChef America.

Ramsay's restaurants have been awarded a total of 15 Michelin stars.

344. MARCO PIERRE WHITE

Marco Pierre White is a British celebrity chef, restaurateur and television personality. He was born on 11th December, 1961. He was born into a family of chefs, so it was no surprise that he chose a career in the professional kitchen.

He left school and went to Hotel St. George to train. In 1987, he opened Harvey's in London, which earned him his first Michelin star. He was awarded three Michelin stars by the time he was 33. He was the youngest person to accomplish this.

He soon gained a name for himself and was attracting young talent like Gordon Ramsay and Curtis Stone. He is known for his contribution to modern international cuisine. He is also known as the first celebrity chef.

His lack of fear for the rules and bold, unprecedented method of running his kitchens have caused some people to call him the "Godfather of Modern Cooking".

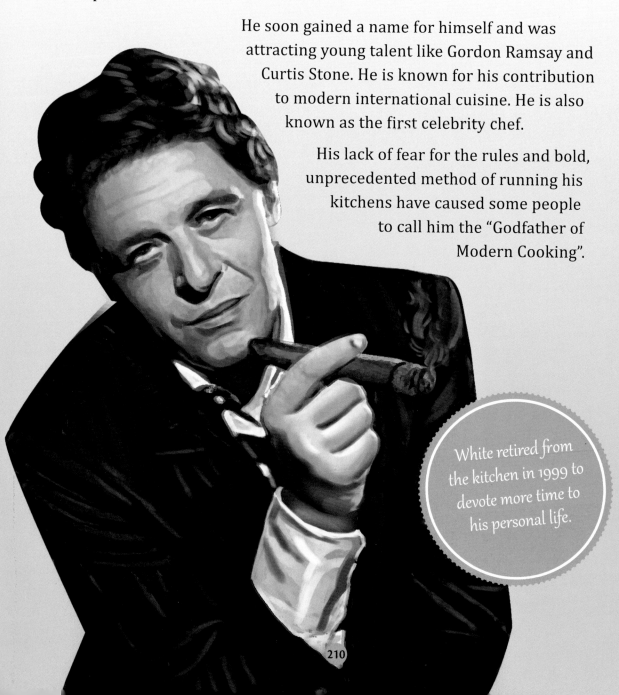

White retired from the kitchen in 1999 to devote more time to his personal life.

345. MARIO BATALI

Mario Batali is an American chef, writer, restaurateur and media personality. He was born on 19th September, 1960, in Washington, USA. Batali started studying at Le Cordon Bleu, but he soon dropped out and began an apprenticeship in London. After completing that, he opened a restaurant, Babbo, in New York. The restaurant received "The Best New Restaurant" Award from the James Beard Foundation. He is also an expert on the history and culture of Italian cuisine. He has continued to open multiple restaurants and write many books.

346. MATT PRESTON

Matt Preston is a British-Australian food journalist, restaurant critic, writer and television personality. He was born on 2nd July, 1961. He is best known as a judge on Network Ten's MasterChef Australia and for his weekly food column in the Taste supplement available in the "Herald Sun", "The Courier-Mail" and "The Daily Telegraph" (Australia) newspapers. Preston is also a writer for MasterChef as well as the former columnist for the food section of "The Age" newspaper's food section, for "Epicure" and "Vogue Entertaining + Travel". Preston was the Creative Director of the Melbourne Food and Wine Festival until 2009.

347. MADHUR JAFFREY

Madhur Jaffrey was born on 13ᵗʰ August, 1933 in Delhi. She is an Indian actress, active in radio, theatre, television and film; she is also a food writer, authoring several cookbooks. Additionally, she is an entrepreneur who, with her acclaimed performances in films such as *Shakespeare Wallah, Six Degrees of Separation* and *Heat and Dust*, introduced the western world to many Indian cuisines. She studied at Miranda House, University of Delhi; after college, she worked for All India Radio. Later, she attended the Royal Academy of Dramatic Art (RADA), from which she graduated with honours in 1957.

Jaffrey is the noted author of cookbooks of Indian, Asian and global vegetarian cuisines. Many of these books have gone on to become bestsellers and many have won the James Beard Foundation awards. She has hosted several *cookery* series on television, including *Madhur Jaffrey's Indian* Cookery in 1982, Madhur Jaffrey's *Far Eastern Cookery* in 1989 and *Madhur Jaffrey's Flavours of India* in 1995. Interestingly, she did not cook at all as she was growing up in Delhi. She had never been in the kitchen and nearly failed cooking at school.

In 1966, an article about Jaffrey and her cooking appeared in the New York Times, because of which she received a book contract that produced *An Invitation to Indian Cooking,* her first book.

348. CURTIS STONE

Curtis Stone is an Australian celebrity chef. He was born on 4th November, 1975, in Melbourne, Australia. At first, he cooked at The Savoy Hotel's 5-star restaurant in Melbourne. He then decided to leave his job and travel through Europe with his best friend. Eventually, he reached London— unemployed and broke. Wanting to gain experience, he volunteered to work for free for the famous chef, Marco Pierre White. Eventually, he was hired and made a name for himself. He went on to become a chef, best-selling author and co-host of "Bravo's Top Chef Masters" and "Around the World in 80 Plates".

349. JOHN CADBURY

John Cadbury is the founder of the chocolate business that was eventually named after him. He was born on 12th August, 1802, in England. He had nine brothers and sisters. The Cadbury manufacturing business was born in 1831, when John Cadbury decided to start producing chocolate on a commercial scale and bought a four-storey warehouse in the nearby Crooked Lane.

This company went on to become one of the world's largest chocolate producers. Cadbury invented the chocolate bar as we know it today. He died on 11th May, 1889.

Fabulous Fashionistas

This section focusses on people who have laid out the materials for modern clothing. Their work has majorly contributed to the fashion industry. Let us find out about their inventions and developments as well as about their lives. Read on and get to know these fashionable stalwarts.

350. CHRISTIAN DIOR

Christian Dior was a French designer and the founder of the eponymous fashion house. Born on 21st January, 1905, in a small town in France, he started out by selling fashion sketches outside his house. In 1941, he began working at a Parisian fashion house.

By 1946, the war had just ended and the atmosphere was hopeful. Dior established his own fashion house. His very first collection showcased what critics dubbed as the "New Look".

His use of rich, opulent fabrics to create form-flattering clothes was well-appreciated. This collection went down in history and catapulted his fashion house to fame. His work was often flaunted by celebrities and royals, a trend that continues even today.

He died suddenly on 24th October, 1957 while on vacation in Tuscany, Italy.

351. GIORGIO ARMANI

Born on 11th July, 1934, in Italy, Giorgio Armani is an iconic fashion designer, primarily known for the "power suits" that he designed for men.

By working as a salesperson at a Milan department store, Armani gained experience about the fashion industry and its working. He then became a designer for menswear at the Nino Cerruti company. He quickly soared to popularity and, by 1975, he had launched his own fashion label.

Armani went on to introduce many new lines like the Armani Jeans and Armani Junior. But the most revolutionary line was the Emporio Armani line, which made his stylish designs accessible at lower prices.

In order to publicise his Emporio Armani line, he resorted to unconventional advertising methods like designing clothes for TV shows and films. He was also the first designer to promote a healthy body image among his models by refusing to employ people with a lower than healthy BMI. In 2007, he teamed up with Samsung to design the Giorgio Armani phone.

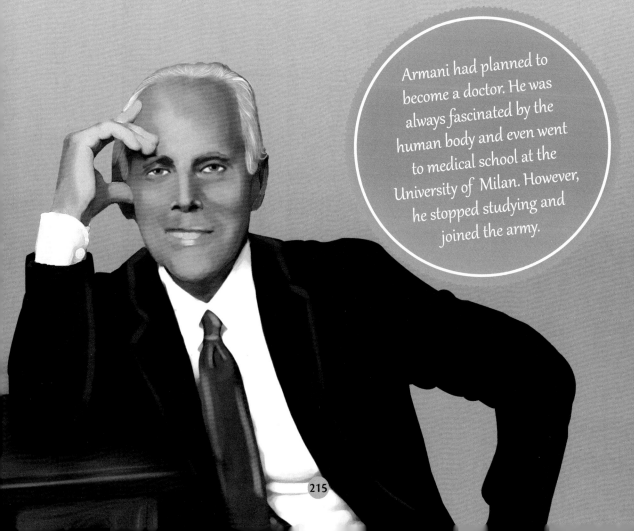

Armani had planned to become a doctor. He was always fascinated by the human body and even went to medical school at the University of Milan. However, he stopped studying and joined the army.

352. CHARLES LEWIS TIFFANY

Charles Tiffany, the founder of American jewellery chain "Tiffany & Co.", was born on 15th February, 1812, in Connecticut, USA. In 1837, along with his school friend John Young, he began a shop named "Tiffany & Young". At the time, they sold stationery and gift items. Slowly, they ventured into glassware, cutlery, clocks and jewellery.

A third partner entered in 1841 and the shop's offering evolved. They sold only the finest, top-quality products. They also began making their own jewellery. Tiffany bought his partners' shares in the shop in 1853 and renamed it to "Tiffany & Co."

By 1868, Tiffany had four stores in locations including London and Paris. This has now increased to over 200. He is also credited with inventing the retail catalogue, which allows customers to view and select designs from a brochure. He died on 18th February, 1902.

353. PIERRE CARDIN

Pierre Cardin was an Italian born French designer. He was born on 7th July, 1922. He was one of the pioneers in the area of high fashion for men. Pierre's father was a wealthy merchant who wanted his son to study architecture. But Pierre was interested in dressmaking. He opened a shop of his own in 1950 and slowly gained a reputation as a men's suit maker. He was the first designer to present ready-to-wear collections. He was also the first to licence his name on a variety of products, like sunglasses.

354. HUBERT DE GIVENCHY

Born on 21st February, 1927, Count Hubert James Marcel Taffin de Givenchy is a French aristocrat, designer and founder of "The House of Givenchy."

Givenchy studied art at the École des Beaux-Arts in Paris and later studied law. After attending the 1937 World's Fair in Paris, he was inspired to work in fashion design. He worked for various leading designers. In 1952, he opened his own house and maintained very low overhead costs in order to lower the prices of his designs. Givenchy's first collection, featuring flawlessly detailed separates, high-style coats and elegant ball gowns, gained immediate international recognition. His first collection was named after actress Bettina Graziani and included the famous "Bettina Blouse".

He was the designer for celebrities like Jacqueline Kennedy and Audrey Hepburn, who wore his designs for many of her films, including the cult hit *Breakfast At Tiffany's*.

In 1957, along with famed Spanish designer Cristóbal Balenciaga, he introduced the "sack silhouette."

355. LOUIS VUITTON

We all know Louis Vuitton as a luxury leather and lifestyle brand and not a person. But there certainly was a founder—he was born almost 200 years ago on 4th August, 1821. In 1852, Vuitton was hired as a box-maker and packer for Emperor Napoleon's wife. This royal employment gave him access to a very elite clientele. He would use the finest material available to create products for them. Vuitton passed away on 27th February, 1892. But his legacy continues to this day, as the brand sells high-quality luxury products.

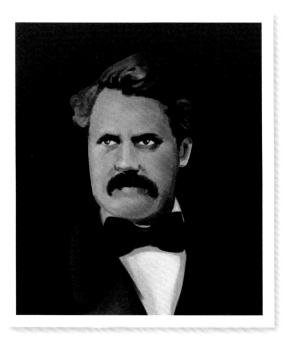

356. COCO CHANEL

French fashion designer Coco Chanel is one of the biggest fashion icons of all time. She was born as Gabrielle Bonheur Chanel on 19th August, 1883, in Saumur, France. After the death of her mother, Chanel was sent to an orphanage, where she learnt how to sew. She got the nickname "Coco" during her short-lived career as a cabaret singer. Chanel picked up hat-making and opened her own hat shop in 1910. By the 1920s, she had already launched her signature perfume "Chanel No. 5" and "Little Black Dress". She died on 10th January, 1971, in Paris.

357. YVES SAINT LAURENT

Yves Saint Laurent was a French fashion designer who was born on 1ˢᵗ August, 1936, in Oran, Algeria. At the age of 16, Saint Laurent entered his designs into a contest and won first place. This inspired him to take up a career in fashion.

He moved to Paris at the age of 18 and attended fashion school, where he soon shot to popularity. Later, Saint Laurent joined the Dior house of fashion. A few years later, Christian Dior passed away. Thus, the title of head designer fell upon the shoulders of the young Saint Laurent, who was a mere 21 years old at the time.

In that year, Dior launched their spring collection that was designed by Saint Laurent. This collection catapulted him to fame and brought great riches and recognition to the Dior house of fashion, which previously was not doing very well. However, Saint Laurent dealt a blow when he was conscripted into the French Army. He suffered a mental breakdown and had to be sent home, only after 20 days of military service.

But this setback did not faze him. By the 1960s, Saint Laurent had started his own company. He was the first designer to come out with a ready-to-wear line, which made his clothes more accessible to the masses. He died in Paris on 1ˢᵗ June, 2008.

Saint Laurent often visited the Majorelle Garden in Morocco, as he found it to be very inspiring. After his death, his ashes were scattered in the garden.

358. RALPH LAUREN

Iconic American designer Ralph Lauren was born as Ralph Lifshitz in New York City on 14th October, 1939. Even though he came from a middle-class Jewish family living in the Bronx, young Lauren would save up his pocket money and buy himself expensive suits.

Instead of taking the academic route, Lauren decided to learn the ropes of the fashion business on the job. Soon, he began designing neckties and selling them to his friends. Not surprisingly, it was neckties that gave him his first break. He established his brand "Polo", which has now expanded to include clothing, perfumes and even furniture.

Lauren also has a humanitarian side. In 2003, the Ralph Lauren Centre for Cancer Care and Prevention was launched in Harlem, New York. He also started the Pink Pony Fund. A percentage of the profits of Pink Pony products are directed towards this fund, which helps in the awareness, treatment and research of breast cancer.

Yet another fund started by Lauren is the American Heroes Fund. This fund awards scholarships to the children of the victims of the World Trade Centre terrorist attack in 2001.

The success of the Polo brand allowed Lauren to purchase an admirable collection of rare, classic cars. He has over 70 of them!

359. MARIO PRADA

Mario Prada was the founder and original designer of the Italian fashion label Prada, a label that creates high-fashion goods for men and women. He started the label with his Martino Prada as a leather goods shop in 1913.

Mario felt that women should not have a role in the business world. He prevented female members of his family from entering his company. However, Mario's son did not want to work for the label, so Mario's daughter, Luisia Prada, took over from Mario and ran the business for almost 20 years.

Prada started its business by making bags and suitcases. These were a huge success, which led to the designing and launch of the first ready-to-wear Prada collection. Its clean lines, classic colours and luxury fabrics made it a huge success.

Prada was known for being ahead of its time during the 1990s. It had an ultramodern industrial sleekness which placed it apart from the other fashion brands of the time. Mario Prada died in 1958.

Mario did not want his company to be run by the women in his family. But his son had no interest in the family business, so it was taken over by his daughter and, later, his granddaughter. Mario's granddaughter, Miuccia, took over the family business from her mother in 1978, when the company was going through a financial struggle.

360. GIANNI VERSACE

Gianni Versace was a top Italian fashion designer, who enjoyed great success during the 1980s and 1990s. He was born on 2nd December, 1946, in Reggio di Calabria, Italy. As his mother was a seamstress, Gianni and his siblings, Santo and Donatella were always exposed to clothes and fashion.

1978 marked the year that Versace opened his first boutique in Milan. His bold designs often received harsh criticism, but Versace was unfazed. He held flamboyant fashion shows that were attended by the who's who of the fashion world. The models were so highly paid and respected that they were called "supermodels". This is why Versace is said to have revolutionised the fashion industry.

He continued to add to his fashion empire, expanding into home furnishings and perfumes. He died on 15th July, 1997.

At the time of his death, Versace's company was worth more than 800 million US dollars.

Versace was tragically shot to death at the age of 50 by a serial killer. It was a big blow to the fashion world and many people believe that he was at the peak of his career when the tragedy occurred.

361. VERA WANG

Chinese-born American fashion designer, Vera Wang, is well-renowned for her beautiful wedding dresses. She was born on 27th June, 1949, in New York City. Despite having no formal training in fashion design, she became the senior fashion editor for Vogue magazine in 1970. She then worked with Ralph Lauren for two years before carving a niche of her own. Wang has designed wedding gowns for celebrities like Victoria Beckham, Jennifer Lopez and Mariah Carey. She has also made figure skating costumes for professional skaters.

362. DONNA KARAN

Donna Karan is an American designer, who is known for the simple, comfortable design of her clothes. She was born on 2nd October, 1948. Her father was a tailor and her mother was a model. She attended Parsons School of Design, but dropped out in 1968 and started working for sportswear designer, Anne Klein. In 1984, she launched her own line, the Donna Karan Co., which eventually became DKNY. In 2004, she received a Lifetime Achievement Award from the Council of Fashion Designers of America.

363. DOLCE AND GABBANA

Dolce and Gabbana is an Italian luxury fashion house that was started by Dominico Dolce and Stefano Gabbana. Dolce was born on 13th August, 1958 and Gabbana was born on 14th November, 1962. The two met in Milan in 1980 and worked for the same fashion house. In 1982, they established a designer consulting studio; in time, it grew to become "Dolce & Gabbana". They presented their first women's collection in 1985 in Milan, where a year later, their store opened its doors.

364. CHRISTIAN LOUBOUTIN

Christian Louboutin is a renowned French footwear designer. He was born on 7th January, 1964, in Paris, France. Blessed with a vivid imagination, Louboutin first started sketching footwear in his early teens. At the age of 18, he got a job with shoe designer Charles Jourdan and continued to work with big names. In 1991, Louboutin launched his own company. By 1993, he had designed his legendary shoes with red soles, which went on to become his trademark. Today, the Louboutin brand also includes handbags and men's shoes.

365. ALEXANDER MCQUEEN

Alexander McQueen was a British designer known for his groundbreaking clothes and precise tailoring. He was born on 17th March, 1969. He was one of six sons of a cab driver. He left school at the age of 16 and was employed at London's Anderson and Sheppard, where he tailored suits for Mikhail Gorbachev and Prince Charles. He enrolled at the fashion college, Central Saint Martins, in 1990. There, he staged a show for his master's thesis, which caught the eye of Isabella Blow, a London stylist. She bought his entire collection!

In 1992, McQueen debuted with a pair of trousers that redefined the traditional cut of the garment. They were pants cut so low that they revealed the cleavage of the backside. This brought him instant media recognition. He later took over as the head designer of Givenchy, a phenomenal achievement for someone only 28 years old!

In 2001, he departed the House of Givenchy and began to diversify his brand to include fragrances (2003), a menswear collection (2004), for which the British Fashion Council named him British Menswear Designer of the Year and McQ (2006), a more affordable ready-to-wear line. He was found dead on 11th February, 2010.

Index

1. A. R. Rahman — 198
2. ABBA — 197
3. Abraham Lincoln — 36
4. Adolf Hitler — 42
5. Agatha Christie — 151
6. Akira Kurosawa — 122
7. Alain Ducasse — 207
8. Albert Einstein — 17
9. Albrecht Altdorfer — 166
10. Alexander Bogomazov — 176
11. Alexander Fleming — 18
12. Alexander Graham Bell — 13
13. Alexander McQueen — 225
14. Alexander the Great — 24
15. Alfred Hitchcock — 114
16. Alfred Nobel — 1
17. Andre Agassi — 104
18. Andrew Stanton — 134
19. Andy Warhol — 169
20. Ansel Adams — 165
21. Anthony Bourdain — 208
22. Antoni Gaudi — 173
23. Aristotle — 83
24. Arthur Conan Doyle — 145
25. Aryabhata — 14
26. Ashoka — 25
27. Asma Jahangir — 78
28. Audrey Hepburn — 126
29. Auguste Rodin — 172
30. Aung San Suu Kyi — 77
31. Aurobindo Ghosh — 93
32. Barack Obama — 45
33. Bartolomeo Scappi — 200
34. Beethoven — 194
35. Benazir Bhutto — 46
36. Benito Mussolini — 41
37. Benjamin Franklin — 7
38. Bill Gates — 64
39. Bob Dylan — 188
40. Bob Marley — 190
41. Botticelli — 160
42. Charles Babbage — 8
43. Charles Darwin — 10
44. Charles de Gaulle — 43
45. Charles Dickens — 142
46. Charles Goodyear — 3
47. Charles Lewis Tiffany — 216
48. Charlie Chaplin — 115
49. Che Guevara — 74
50. Chen Guangcheng — 81
51. Christian Dior — 214
52. Christian Louboutin — 224
53. Clara Barton — 69
54. Claude Monet — 171
55. Coco Chanel — 218
56. Confucius — 85
57. Constantine — 27
58. Curtis Stone — 213
59. Cyrus the Great — 24
60. D. W. Griffith — 116
61. Dan Brown — 157
62. Dante Alighieri — 137
63. David Beckham — 107
64. David Bowie — 191
65. David Hume — 88
66. Desmond Tutu — 75
67. Dhirubhai Ambani — 58
68. Diego Maradona — 97
69. Dolce and Gabbana — 224
70. Don Bradman — 96
71. Donald Trump — 52
72. Donatello — 161
73. Donna Karan — 223
74. Edgar Allan Poe — 141
75. Édouard Manet — 180
76. Edvard Munch — 175
77. Eleanor Roosevelt — 70
78. Ellen Sirleaf — 76
79. Elton John — 191
80. Elvis Presley — 187
81. Emily Dickinson — 143
82. Eminem — 198
83. Enid Blyton — 153
84. Eratosthenes of Cyrene — 11
85. Ernest Hemmingway — 152
86. Ezra Pound — 150
87. F. Scott Fitzgerald — 152
88. Federico Fellini — 125
89. Fidel Castro — 51
90. Florence Nightingale — 72
91. Francis Bacon — 138
92. Francois Truffaut — 127
93. Frank Gehry — 181
94. Frank Sinatra — 184
95. Franklin Roosevelt — 41
96. Frantz Fanon — 74
97. Franz Marc — 176
98. Freddie Mercury — 190
99. Frederic Auguste Bartholdi — 170
100. Galileo Galilei — 9
101. Genghis Khan — 29
102. Georg Wilhelm Friedrich Hegel — 90
103. George Bernard Shaw — 145
104. George Crum — 201
105. George Eliot — 143
106. George Lucas — 128
107. George Orwell — 154
108. George Washington — 33
109. Georges Melies — 119
110. Gian Lorenzo Bernini — 163
111. Gianni Versace — 222
112. Giorgio Armani — 215
113. Giorgio Vasari — 163
114. Gordon Ramsay — 209
115. Gregory Peck — 124
116. Guglielmo Marconi — 16
117. Gustav Klimt — 175
118. Gustave Eiffel — 168
119. Harriet Tubman — 68
120. Helen Keller — 68
121. Henri Cartier-Bresson — 179
122. Henri Nestlé — 201
123. Henry Ford — 53
124. Henry VIII — 31
125. Herge — 156
126. Hubert de Givenchy — 217
127. Humphrey Bogart — 118
128. Immanuel Kant — 89
129. Indira Gandhi — 50
130. Indra Nooyi — 59
131. Ingmar Bergman — 124
132. Irvine Robbins and Burton Baskin — 205
133. Isaac Newton — 6
134. J F Kennedy — 51
135. J S Mill — 90
136. J. K. Rowling — 158
137. J. R. R. Tolkien — 151
138. Jack Nicklaus — 98
139. Jackson Pollock — 179
140. James Beard — 203
141. James Brown — 186
142. James Cameron — 130
143. James Watt — 8
144. Jamie Oliver — 199
145. Jane Austen — 140
146. Jawaharlal Nehru — 43
147. Jean-Jacques Rousseau — 89
148. Jean-Luc Godard — 126
149. Jeff Bezos — 61
150. Jesse Owens — 107

OTHER TITLES IN THIS SERIES

ISBN: 978-81-87107-46-0

ISBN: 978-93-52760-95-4

ISBN: 978-93-84225-31-5

ISBN: 978-93-80070-79-7

ISBN: 978-81-87107-58-3

ISBN: 978-93-52764-06-8

ISBN: 978-93-83202-81-2

ISBN: 978-93-80069-36-4

ISBN: 978-81-87107-52-1

ISBN: 978-81-87107-57-6

ISBN: 978-93-81607-57-2

ISBN: 978-93-52760-96-1

ISBN: 978-81-87107-53-8

ISBN: 978-93-80070-84-1

ISBN: 978-93-80070-83-4

ISBN: 978-81-87107-55-2

ISBN: 978-93-81607-49-7

ISBN: 978-81-87107-56-9